A Generation of Excellence

Vaughn J. Featherstone

A Generation of Excellence

A GUIDE FOR PARENTS AND YOUTH LEADERS

Vaughn J. Featherstone

BOOKCRAFT, INC.

Salt Lake City, Utah

Library of Congress Catalog Card Number: 75-34833

ISBN 0-88494-292-9

5th Printing, 1986

LITHOGRAPHED IN U.S.A. BY
PUBLISHERS PRESS
SALT LAKE CITY, UTAH

CONTENTS

FOREWORD

Vaughn J. Featherstone is unusually well equipped to write this book. In his youth he experienced many of the needs and urges our young folk manifest today — the need to belong, the urge to *be* someone, for example. Since the Church helped to meet his needs then, he knows it will do the same for today's youth.

His later experiences confirm this conviction. Blessed with a talent for working with the youth and a firm resolve to develop it, in numerous Church callings even before being called to the Presiding Bishopric he has had great success in influencing young persons in the direction of successful, happy living. Several examples of this are reflected in personal stories included in this book.

When initially approached, the author was somewhat reticent about preparing this book. To be valid, it must be written around his experiences in the area of youth leadership. He was particularly concerned lest he should appear to be aggrandizing himself, yet it was clear that the message would not come across without personal examples. He was finally prevailed upon to trust the LDS reader to place the correct interpretation on his personal allusions.

Parents and other leaders of youth, as well as young people with the innate urge to achieve, will share the publisher's enthusiasm for this book. In it they will find the simple, straightforward guidance of one who has successfully trodden the road, both as a youth and an adult. And they will see with clarity that the same kind of success can be theirs.

THE PUBLISHER

PREFACE

It was shortly after I got married that I was impressed with the thought that we can increase our contribution by sharpening our focus. I could profitably do this, I reflected, in my Church service.

Many areas of Church activity interested me — genealogy, Scouting, teaching, the welfare program, youth, missionary work (this one particularly, since I had not served a mission). In which one if any should I specialize? After several months of reflection, my thoughts crystallized around work with the youth of the Church. Here it seemed was where the Lord wanted my major contribution.

That this was the right decision has been demonstrated by the fact that since that time virtually all my calls to Church service have been youth oriented. Twice a Scoutmaster, MIA superintendent at both stake and ward levels, service in several other stake MIA positions, explorer post adviser, priesthood quorum adviser, member of a bishopric, high councilor assigned to youth work, member of the general YMMIA board and of the Church General Priesthood Missionary Committee — even on my two stake missions (one as stake mission president) I was able through organizing successful youth missionary committees to sustain this most enjoyable and I hope effective association with the youth. And as president of the Boise North Stake I was blessed to bring an emphasis on youth programs which substantially lifted the levels of youth activity in the stake. I treasure the memories of the involvement with the young people which these callings have brought me.

And now, as a member of the Presiding Bishopric, I again have the opportunity of serving the youth of the Church. Indeed, the First Presidency has stated, and the current President of the Church has reaffirmed, that the Presiding Bishopric's first and foremost responsibility is the Aaronic Priesthood youth — meaning, of course, both young men and young women of that age level. It is the Presiding Bishopric's pleasant task to initiate and promote programs which, when implemented by dedicated parents and local leaders, will not only get our young men ready for missions and the Melchizedek Priesthood but will help to prepare our young men and women for a life of joy such as the Lord intended for them — celestial marriage and all that it entails in terms of home and family here and hereafter, the temporal and spiritual success which only the gospel of Jesus Christ can bring to a life. In the process we will be preparing a generation that will astonish the world.

The present generation of youth may well be the one which makes the final preparations for the Savior's second coming. More than ever this underlines the sacred trust we have as parents and leaders of LDS youth to ensure that no young person under our stewardship is lost through any lack of effort on our part.

That stewardship is not always easy to fulfill. Aids along the way are welcome. While this book is in no way a Church-sponsored publication but is solely my individual responsibility, it is the outcome of the experience the Lord has blessed me with in this field. As such it is my hope that the book will in some way assist others in their stewardship.

1
HELP THEM
TO CHOOSE

Our youth have their free agency to make choices — for good or otherwise. But their choices will be better ones if we teach them the consequences not only of sin, but of service.

Ardeth Kapp, teaching a group of young people at a weekend conference, divided them into two groups of fifty. She had the first group, which sat right with the other one, close their eyes, then she wrote on the blackboard the words *orange, apple, banana, pear,* and so forth for the others to see. She then erased these words from the board, had the second group close their eyes, and wrote the words *sex, kissing, petting, adultery,* for the first group to see. She then erased the words.

With both groups open-eyed, she next wrote on the blackboard "r-pe" and asked what the word was. To the first group, the word was *ripe.* The other group supposed, quite naturally, that the word was *rape.* In that brief demonstration Ardeth showed the young people how they can indeed be conditioned by practically everything that comes into their minds — by TV, by the music they listen to, by the movies they see.

The stimuli, of course, influence our youth in making

choices. But are they the *right* choices? This is where we come in. It is the responsibility of the adult leader to help our youth understand why it is so vital to make the right choices. We do a great disservice by suggesting a course of action without teaching why, without "telling it like it is." To expect blind obedience without sharing the possible results of different choices is folly on the part of the adult leader. Our youth need to know. They must have facts and information. They must have an understanding so that they can judge for themselves, running various alternatives through their own mental processes and thus making decisions based on facts rather than just on direction.

Our young people in this generation have been given a straight dose by Satan. He blatantly sells his wares without disguise or costume. He boldly and basely presents his product, his philosophy of life. His wares are so common that even the very protected have been exposed.

As part of the divine counterbalance, we need to let the youth know of Satan's plan and how it will destroy them. We need to teach them why it is so vital to follow the prophet, why living a clean, virtuous, modest life will bring happiness, joy and security.

I read two case histories related by a professor of social work which graphically illustrate "the way it is" for those who, unwittingly or otherwise, choose Satan.

> A fifteen-year-old girl writes about her runaway experience, indicating the dual feeling of wanting to be mothered, while fighting for independence and sophistication: "The first night was cold, and walking around the avenues we could mock the [soliciting women]. The big man and his badge would give us a cold eye and without hesitation we would make a [foul gesture]. I wished for my mother and I wished for sympathy, for a warm bed, and not the cold shipyard or the park swings. I feel really old for fifteen, there just isn't any place to go. Mama, I miss you and I just spent my last dollar for cigarettes."
>
> In a few more years when she has become hardened to the scenes around her, when she becomes even more severed from

her mother's relationships, when the use of drugs and cigarettes harden her to the core, we will find nothing but misery, and shame, and degradation in this young creation of God.

Case two is the death letter of another young lady:

> Dear ....: I have gone to find peace, love and quiet without hate. You have not had the time to glance at a single ray of beauty or say a kind word. Please don't cry, which would be very hard for you to do anyway. If you want these things you will find [them] at the end of the rainbow.

But the process of degradation, even if it has ensnared our youth, need not be irreversible. Even after major problems connected with poor choices, our youth can indeed turn the corner and begin making *good* choices — if they are taught *how*.

At a youth conference, a girl of about twenty who had just closed the meeting with prayer came up to me. "Bishop Featherstone," she said, "I am immoral!" She said it loud enough that several around might have heard her. I was somewhat taken aback and I quietly said to her, "You get to your bishop and discuss the matter with him." I did it out of a sense of love and feeling, and she knew that I was interested in her.

A few days later I received a letter from her. It went something like this: "Dear Bishop Featherstone: I am the girl who closed the meeting with prayer. At the close of the conference I told you that I was immoral. That was true. I have slept in bed with married men overnight. I have petted heavily. I knew these things were wrong but I never felt sorry for them until this morning. For the first time in my life I had a spiritual experience. I have visited with my bishop and asked him to hold a Church court. I expect to be excommunicated, but I know this is what it will take to receive forgiveness and truly repent. Thank you, Bishop Featherstone. Thank you so much for helping me."

Now this young lady was on her way to changing her life.

In the Beatitudes as listed in Third Nephi, chapter 12, the Savior said, "Blessed are the poor in spirit." And then he added the words to the Nephites, "who come unto me" before finishing, "for theirs is the kingdom of heaven."

After a period of immorality this young woman had finally chosen to come to Christ. She didn't yet know the repentance process; she was just beginning. But after she had mourned enough and suffered enough, the sin and the transgressions could be purged from her life through repentance. She could then learn to love the Savior with every particle of her being.

The great thing we need to teach our young people, apart from self-discipline, is to expect just consequences in this "game" of choices. The consequence of the correct choices is of course the reward of eternal life from a sweet Heavenly Father.

Someone once wrote the standards of a good man, a set of choices for life:

> For working most of my living time, I want more than money. I want respect. I am resolved to earn that respect, since there is no other way that any man can obtain respect except by earning it. I want my character and my abilities to improve while I am at work. If I fail to strengthen myself during worktime I will surely be less satisfied in the time I spend with my family, my friends, and my church. My happiness in life depends upon the high standards I set for myself at work. I want whatever I earn, but I do not expect others to pay me until after I have given them honest value. I will not be a parasite or make other humans poorer by failing to do my job well.

Each of us as parents or other adult leaders has learned the value of making good choices in Church, community, country, work-a-day activities — and most importantly in our families. Our job is to share what we have learned so that our youth don't have to learn by misadventure.

By contrast to those who have made unfortunate choices and who have had to suffer grave consequences is a woman who came to my office. She is totally pure, though divorced for many years due to the fault of her husband. In all those twenty-five years since she has been divorced, she has never read a story or a book that even approached the subject of sexual promiscuity. She has resigned from several secretarial positions because bosses expected a compromise; or because they used foul language, and she was not willing to work in a place where that kind of language was used. She has self-respect. She has courage like few women I know. These come from a totally pure life.

When you are clean and morally pure, you fear no man — you make right choices. Understanding this principle will help our youth to make a decision to be pure, to have integrity, to have courage, to have a sense of self-worth — all desirable things; far more desirable, I might add, than the attractively packaged wares Satan sells to a young person with unknown drives and passions, unfelt responses in his or her soul. The Lord has a reward so great and so splendid that it will appeal to our youth far above what Satan can offer.

One of the most effective deterrents to Lucifer's plan, of course, is the great law and principle of service. We need to teach and train our youth to make a decision in this life to choose to be of *service* to their fellowmen. The Savior taught in his golden rule that we must love our neighbor as ourselves. It seems that the spirit of the golden rule is an invitation to take the initiative in giving service. Possibly one reason the world sometimes looks dull is that we are so wrapped up in our own affairs that we don't have time to enter into the lives of others. How often do we wait for great opportunities for service, for better health, or some other situation that may never come!

The quiet, well-timed voluntary service graciously given may appear to have little substance, but it is a contribution to both receiver and giver, and is often a resounding affirmation that the right choice has been made.

Richard L. Evans said, "After all, we owe a kind of rent, if we may call it that, or at least an obligation for the space we occupy on earth; for the tenancy and tenure we have here, for the beauty and sustenance, and the privilege of living life."

The value of service was underscored for me as I sat in an Aaronic Priesthood committee meeting in the Church Office Building. A committee member said: "One of my graduate students came in today and said that when he was an Eagle Scout, he had a Scoutmaster who had helped eighteen of the boys in the troop to obtain the rank of Eagle. He said, 'I know my Scoutmaster cared. My particular interest was swimming and diving, and I never entered a swimming meet or a diving meet but that I could always look over to the side and see my Scoutmaster, watching me perform. He was often there when even my parents weren't.' " Then this Aaronic Priesthood committee member added, "We should never lose this concept of focusing on the individual."

I spoke up and said, "I believe in that kind of service with all of my heart and soul," whereupon the committee member responded, "The graduate student I'm talking about was Dennis Gehring. You knew him and his Scoutmaster."

As I talked with the Scoutmaster later, he said: "Dennis was a Scout of mine approximately twenty-two years ago. The love which I felt and still feel for Dennis, the desire I had and still have to see him achieve, has remained with me through these many years. I never expected even the slightest particle of reward for such service, yet the achievements he has made and the appreciation he has been kind enough to express to me have been tremendously rewarding to me."

The rewards for making the choice to serve are not always immediate, but as the Master has said, "Whatsoever a man soweth, that shall he also reap." And again the Bible says, "Cast thy bread upon the waters: for thou shalt find it after many days."

I promise you that as you teach your young people the value of service you can assure them that they can no more do a good thing, perform a service, be a blessing to people, than it will return to bless them hundreds of times over. Service is a creative expression of self. If a person does not give something of himself to others, he dries up, shrinks, shrivels. On the other hand, giving of oneself adds to enjoyment of life, expands areas of interest, gives feelings of participating. It makes one more spiritual and more receptive to the whisperings of the Spirit; it rebuffs Satan. As Longfellow said, "Give what you have to someone. It may be better than you dare to think."

There have been many examples of those who chose to perform heroic service. The life of Albert Schweitzer is a living testimony to the high value he placed on selfless service to society.

The schoolboy who became Lord Byron had a malformation of one foot, and this lameness was the cause of much physical suffering in childhood and of mental anguish throughout his life. When at school he was unable to fight a bully who was beating another boy, Byron offered to take half the blows.

Recall, too, the courage of Horatio in Shakespeare's *Hamlet*. Confronted by the ghost, Horatio (though startled by its appearance) said, "If there be any good thing to be done that may to thee do ease, and grace to me, speak to me."

If our youth are going to be able to walk with their heads high, if they are going to be able to make some new high-water marks and cause a ripple in this great ocean of life, it will be done as they choose to perform service. Service is stimulating, fulfilling, the real worth of life to our young people.

Just as we teach our youth the consequences of sin, so also we should teach them the consequences of good — of service, for example. I do not believe there is a young person in the Church that cannot be appealed to if we properly train him and instruct him by our living example.

Every young person ought to be exposed to the story of Damon and Pythias, ought to have the privilege of reading of the great lives of the leaders in the Church, ought to make a study of service as the Savior applied it in his life and as his disciples have applied it. As we teach service, conversion truly will come to our youth. And those who will play the game of consequences, who choose to follow the principles of Jesus Christ and his gospel, will find that the consequences are sure, predictable, rewarding. To paraphrase the Prophet Joseph Smith, "We should teach our people correct principles and let them govern themselves." This great statement should apply in all things, and especially in working with our young people.

Service, of course, leads directly to the quality of being responsible as our youth climb another rung upward toward true adulthood.

In a Dartnell Corporation booklet I read:

> When man is standing on his own feet he has passed from the dependence of adolescence to the responsibilities of adult citizenship. A person is not mature so long as he continues to try to solve adult problems in childish ways, or to satisfy his ego with adolescent experiences. Maturity involves an intelligent appraisal of disappointments, burned fingers, spoiled pages, and plans that went wrong, as well as a balanced appreciation of successes. One cannot escape the responsibility of maturity by quoting the doctrine of Marx, who held that every man's actions were conditioned by the social class to which he belonged; or the doctrine of Freud, who said that what a man does is subject to prenatal and juvenile influences over which he had no control.

> Responsibility is the inevitable price one has to pay for independence. When an individual is free to act as he likes, he is accountable for what he does. A slave has no responsibility, but as soon as he becomes a free man he participates not only in freedom, but in obligations to himself, his family, his community, and the nation. It is not enough to remain standing; we must evolve. Growth is a characteristic of life, and growth means change. The wise man regards his present situation as only the sketch of a picture which he must finish. If he does not try to do a little more or a little better than he can do easily, he will never learn the rest that he is capable of doing.

Think of that line again: "Responsibility is the inevitable price one has to pay for independence." We should not have an "I-told-you-so" attitude with our youth. We should train, teach, do all we can. As President David

O. McKay said, "There is no greater responsibility in the world than the training of a human soul." Our responsibility is to expose to our young people the havoc, the ruin, the folly, the foolishness of Satan's way. We need to paint the picture so vividly that they will see clearly that the joys and the excitement which Satan portrays in his presentation are his cunning prelude to the slow but sure shackling and chains of everyone who binds himself to Satan.

On the other hand, we should also teach our youth the great goodness of a sweet, kind, loving Heavenly Father who rewards us justly for maintaining our integrity, for choosing correctly, for living the clean life, for working a day's work for an honest day's pay, for serving our fellowmen, for becoming more spiritual.

In the Church we have received a tremendous amount. We have the model through our Savior Jesus Christ. We have great and holy men whose lives are dedicated to service. We have priesthood leaders, bishops, stake presidents, quorum and class leaders. We have fathers who are patriarchs who function and spend their lives in service to their fellowmen. Surely in the Church of Jesus Christ we have an organization more service oriented than any other organization in the world. Why, then, should we not be the prototype for this new and choice generation, bearing our personal witness to the validity of choices based on eternal verities?

With all this behind them, why indeed should we not expect our youth to make the right choices?

2
INSPIRE THEM
TO GREATNESS

There is greatness in each of our youth, and each can experience greatness as measured by the Savior — if as youth leaders we provide the images.

One night shortly after I moved into a new stake I had the opportunity to call on another stake member. I'd been called to a stake mission and this man too was on a stake mission. I was new in this assignment, so we had a lot of things to discuss.

Fairly poor at the time, I had put on the best suit I had and an overcoat which was old and embarrassing to me but needful during the winter months. As I walked into the home, my host, whom I had never before met, came up behind me and helped me take off my coat — something that had never happened in my life. He immediately hung my coat up in the closet, and then we went into a beautifully furnished room. I can recall the atmosphere — and the spiritual feeling — as I walked into his living room where large overstuffed chairs, a beautiful piano, and heavy carpeting adorned the room. Beautiful, tasteful pictures hung on the walls, and lamps of excellent design softly lighted the room. I was thoroughly impressed. We sat down and went through the meeting, discussing our responsibilities as stake missionaries.

When we were through I went over to the closet and searched for my coat. But I couldn't find it. Then I noticed my host standing there behind me with my coat. He held it out and assisted me in putting it on — clumsy as I was, never before having been helped on with my coat.

As I left his home that night, I wanted to be the kind of gentleman he was. I wanted to live the way he lived. This brief, almost casual encounter was to have a great impact upon my life: I had experienced one of those "images of greatness" that would help set a pattern for the kind of man I wanted to be.

Our young people have a similar need. They should see — should experience — patterns which are beyond their normal range of life. They should see a life that is better than they presently have or hope for. They need to be able to see that people can accomplish great things. They ought to read biographies of those who have achieved greatness. Most importantly, they also need to understand that they may achieve greatness as measured by the Savior, by emulating the patterns of true greatness that they see or read about.

Through the years I have collected many excellent materials that form these kinds of images. These materials I have filed, read, and reread — used a hundred times over. Some of them come from personal experiences like my meeting with the stake missionary. Others come from great books, from poems, from articles I have picked up and read while waiting at some airport, from stirring talks by our great Church leaders.

But all the experiences have one thing in common: they form images — word pictures — of greatness. And from the images come exciting visions of broad, lifetime objectives and goals. Youth respond to them. They do this, I suspect, not only because they see a little of themselves in each image, but because they catch an important picture of what is out ahead — if only they will reach.

Our youth may never serve in high places. They may never be in the political arena. They may not be successful financially as appraised by the outside world. But as we and they pattern and mold our lives after the Master, truly every one of them can become great. Self-mastery, self-discipline, self-denial, having the ability to suffer in silence, having charity, love, devotion to the cause, faith, ambition and energy combined with integrity — these are all qualities which every soul can have. These qualities aren't based on intelligence or intellectuality. They are based on conduct of living, and many great men who have applied these character traits have been lifted to heights they would not have believed possible.

It has been my experience to float down the middle fork of the Salmon River many times, often with Scouts and Explorers from our stake. I remember quoting many great scriptures and verses and stories to the young men in my boat, feeling that there on the Salmon I might be teaching them.

One day I recounted the story of *Ben Hur*. I told of Ben Hur's days — even years — in the galleys. I talked of his attitude. I recalled the chariot race and how in that race Messala reached out and lashed at Sheik Ilderim's Arabian horses driven by Ben Hur, and how in one great impulse they leaped forward. And then I discussed how Ben Hur held them in control, as I read to the young men: "Where got Ben Hur the large and mighty grip which helped him now so well? Where but from the oar with which so long he fought the sea. And what was this spring of the floor under his feet to the dizzy eccentric lurch with which in the old time the trembling ship yielded to the beat of staggering billows, drunk with their power. So he kept his place. . . ."

I remember as I quoted these words how very impressed they were. I remember how these young men could tie that story into a living experience through which they were now going as they floated in rafts on the white water of the middle fork of the Salmon. I could often see these young men bend their paddles and oars, causing the muscles to ripple across their backs.

Let me extract from that great book *Ben Hur* by Lew Wallace some of the quotations that have given me a deeper understanding of the human soul and that suggest a pattern to assist us in gaining true greatness.

The book gives one statement about man's quest for truth which I shall never forget: "Like you, my brethren, I went out of the beaten ways, I went where man had not been, where only God was. . . ." That brief statement has caused a hundred thoughts to flash into my mind. I had a great desire to find sacred, holy places — high on a mountain top, in the backwoods, or by a beautiful flowing river where I could communicate with God, as was implied in this statement.

Another brief but beautiful passage early in the book touched me deeply: "The night, like most nights of the winter season in the hill country, was clear, crisp, and sparkling with stars. There was no wind. The atmosphere seemed never so pure, and the stillness was more than silence; it was a holy hush, a warning that heaven was stooping low to whisper good things to the listening earth." Think of the impact such a statement could have on a young person who is searching and seeking for peace.

In another memorable quotation a father, Simonides, describes his daughter: "The Lord hath been good to me in many ways; but thou, Esther, art the sovereign excellence of his favor." A young woman reading this may well find a goal for which she would work. For her father, her bishop, or for someone she prized to say such a thing about her would indeed be a strong motivational factor in her life.

The *spirit* of greatness comes out loud and clear as Simonides, who is responsible for all investments of the Hur family, questions Malluch the servant concerning Ben Hur.

"In what he said or did, Malluch, could you in anywise detect his master-idea?" [Meaning, his main motive for his words and actions.]

"As to that, Master Simonides," Malluch responds, "I can answer with much assurance. He is devoted to finding his mother and sister — that first. Then he has a grievance against Rome; and as the Messala of whom I told you had something to do with the wrong, the great present object is to humiliate him. . . ."

"The Messala is influential," said Simonides, thoughtfully.

"Yes; but the next meeting will be in the Circus."

"Well, and then?"

"The son of Arrius [Ben Hur] will win."

"How know you?"

Malluch smiled.

"I am judging by what he says."

"Is that all?"

"No; there is a much better sign — his spirit."

"Ay; but Malluch, his idea of vengeance — what is its scope? . . . Is his feeling but the vagary of a sensitive boy, or has it the seasoning of suffering manhood to give it endurance?"

Many of us who have worked with young men and women have found youth with great spirit. It's more than what they say, it's a spirit that thunders so loudly that no one can misunderstand.

Recall again with me the words of Ben Hur as he met with Sheik Ilderim and discussed the possibility of riding the sheik's four Arabian white stallions in the circus against Messala:

"Enough!" he said. "If at the roots of thy tongue is a lie in coil, Solomon himself had not been safe against thee. . . . But as to thy skill. What experience hast thou in racing with chariots? And the horses — canst thou make them creatures of thy will . . . to come at call? To go, if thou sayest it, to the last extreme of breath and strength? . . . The gift, my son, is not to everyone. Ah . . . I knew a king who governed millions of men, their perfect master, but could not win the respect of a horse."

And then Ben Hur's response:

"I know now why it is that in the love of an Arab his horse is next to his children; and I know, also, why the Arab horses are the best in the world; but, good sheik, I would not have you judge me by words alone; for, as you know, all promises of men sometimes fail. Give me the trial first on some plain hereabout, and put the four in my hand tomorrow. . . . I tell thee thy sons of the Desert, though they have separately the speed of eagles and the endurance of lions, will fail if they are not trained to run together under the yoke. For bethink thee, Sheik, in every four there is one the slowest and one the swiftest."

Then came the competition between Ben Hur and the four Arabians of Sheik Ilderim against Messala. As we saw earlier, during the race, with the chariots side by side, with lightning quickness Messala reached out and whipped the flesh of the white Arabians that had never to that day felt the whip. But the hardening experience of the galleys gave Ben Hur the ascendancy over even that emergency. "So he kept his place, and gave the four free rein, and called to them in soothing voice, trying merely to guide them round the dangerous turn; and before the fever of the people began to abate, he had back the mastery [and] the sympathy and admiration of every one not a Roman." Ben Hur won the race — the direct result of his *character* as an individual.

Toward the end of the book, Ben Hur's sister Tirzah and her mother have been told that there is one Jesus Christ who can heal them of their leprosy. They hear of the road which Jesus will travel, and they find the road:

> The road at the edge of which the group was posted was little more than a worn path or trail, winding crookedly through tumuli of limestone. If the stranger kept it, he must meet them face to face; and he did so, until near enough to hear the cry she was bound to give. Then, uncovering her head, a further demand of the law, she shouted shrilly, "Unclean, unclean!"
>
> To her surprise, the man came steadily on.
>
> "What would you have?" he asked, stopping opposite them not four yards off.
>
> "Thou seest us. Have a care," the mother said, with dignity.
>
> "Woman, I am the courier of him who but speaketh but once to such as thou and they are healed. I am not afraid."
>
> "The Nazarene?"
>
> "The Messiah," he said.
>
> "Is it true that he cometh to the city today?"
>
> "He is now at Bethphage."
>
> "On what road, master?"

"This one."

She clasped her hands, and looked up thankfully.

"For whom takest thou him?" the man asked, with pity.

"The Son of God," she replied.

"Stay thou here then; or, as there is a multitude with him, take thy stand by the rock yonder, the white one under the tree, and as he goeth by fail not to call to him; call, and fear not. If thy faith but equal thy knowledge, he will hear thee though all the heavens thunder."

What a message for a young person to get! What a thrilling story! Just as the inspiration came to Lew Wallace and he put on paper those beautiful words, I am sure they would thrill every young soul as they did me as I first read them. We can indeed give our youth vicarious experiences of greatness which will help them to achieve that which they are destined to become.

Along with vicarious experiences, we also have first-hand experiences we might call images of example, which sometimes surge into our lives and make an impact that changes us forever. Such was the case with the playwright Moss Hart in his early youth. He gives us a vivid account of that turning point in his life.

After the death of his Aunt Kate, who had exposed him to as much greatness, culture and experience as her limited funds would allow, he returned home from the funeral. The following excerpt[1] from his book *Act One* records the feelings he had at that time.

I have always experienced my grief privately, and then it was done. The funeral has always left me unmoved. Such rites as I have attended, I have attended unwillingly and only as a mark of respect to the living and not to the dead. I have said my goodbyes unpublicly. . . . It was a long walk to where Aunt Kate lay buried. . . . The cemetery did not seem an unpleasant place to be after the subway. It was almost a spring-like day for

[1]From *Act One*, by Moss Hart. Copyright © 1959 by Catherine Carlisle Hart and Joseph M. Hyman, Trustees. Reprinted by permission of Random House, Inc.

the middle of winter, and though the trees were leafless, the well-kept lawns around the graves were a sparkling green. I came to the end of a little path and there in front of me was the grave of my aunt, some of the funeral greens still upon it. Next to it was the grave of my grandfather.

I stood there not knowing quite what to do. I had been impelled to come here by some force within me of terrible urgency, but now that I was here I did not know what to do. I could think only that here were the two people whose lives had meant the most to mine and what a pitiful waste their lives had been to themselves. They were both better, I knew, than life had allowed them to be; and standing there I thought of them more clearly than I ever had before. Fleeting words and moments with both of them came back to me with startling clarity and I suddenly realized how much of their hopes had been unconsciously pinned on me. I had been their bulwark against complete defeat. Far from feeling sorrow or self-pity I began to shake with an uncontrollable rage. To take a job as a shipping clerk or errand boy was no worse than hundreds of boys my own age and circumstances were doing every day of the week. But standing by the graves of my aunt and my grandfather, I was damned if I would. For all that they had been to me, I owed it to them not to; and out of my rage I resolved that come what may, I was sticking to the theater and I would never turn back. And the truth of the matter is that from that actual moment on, I never did.

Moss Hart knew that he was meant to be something greater and nobler — he had seen an image of example. Our personal examples of such important turning-places or pivot-places in our lives are vital to the youth as we teach them, share with them. As leaders of youth, let us not be receptacles but rather transfer agents, sharing the great experiences of our lives.

Every day we see examples that teach us greatness, if our eyes are open. The news media are full of them; there are the obscure heroes that come into our real-life experience; there are occurrences on a schoolground or in a classroom where experiences that are never recorded take place.

For example, sitting in a Denver airport a few years ago I remember picking up the newspaper and reading a question-and-answer column by Hy Gardner:

Question: "Back when Jackie Robinson joined the Brooklyn Dodgers, is it true the other players threatened to go out on strike unless he was dropped? If so, what happened?"

Answer: "Breaking the color barrier in baseball, Jackie's presence was resented not only by many of the Brooklyn teammates, but by other players throughout the league. Ford Frick, the National League president, spiked the strike threat by issuing this momentous statement: 'If you do this you will be suspended from the league. I do not care if half the league strikes. Those who do it will encounter quick retribution. All will be suspended and I don't care if it wrecks the National League. This is the United States of America, and one citizen has just as much right to play as another.' "

And thus we saw a man loom to greatness — we saw an image of example.

Another powerful image is the image of perfection. The sculptor Michelangelo, having lost his eyesight at ninety, ran his hands over a statue in St. Peter's cathedral and exclaimed, "I still learn." What a sobering thought for a young person to catch a vision of humility and perfection as exemplified in one of the greatest artists of all time.

One way for our youth to associate with greatness is to polish their minds against the minds of others. As they read about Michelangelo, about William James, about the General Authorities of the Church, about the very pinnacle, the Savior himself, they can polish their minds against perfection or at least excellence.

Dull men have often been known to brush aside the study of the lives of successful men because the "same conditions" do not apply to them. Perhaps that is why they are dull. The usefulness of biography lies in the fact that in every man there is something we may learn to advantage. We can learn without hardship, without repeating errors, without the loss of time involved in experimenting on our own.

Another image of perfection I shall never forget concerns a famous artist who painted a great picture — the finest work he'd ever done. But one day he was found weeping beside his masterpiece. "What is the trouble?" he was asked. "Aren't you satisfied with the picture?"

"Yes," he replied, "that's just the trouble; I *am* satisfied."

He knew that, being satisfied, he would never do better work. His ambition would wane, he would begin to slip, and his future would no longer be a period of increasing greatness as an artist. What a brilliant lesson this is for a young person!

We go to Victor Hugo for an example of another important image — the image of challenge. He wrote:

> For there are many great deeds in the small struggles of life. There is a determined though unseen bravery which defends itself foot to foot in the darkness against the fatal invasions of necessity and of baseness — noble and mysterious triumph which no eye sees, which no renown rewards, which no flourish or triumph salutes. Life's misfortunes, isolation, abandonment, poverty, are battlefields which have their heroes — obscure heroes sometimes greater than the illustrious heroes. Strong and rare natures are thus created. . . . Distress is the nurse of self-respect; misfortune is a good breast for great souls.

While flying into Atlanta on one occasion, I was reminded of another image our young people need to meet — the image of courage. Reading through the *New Yorker* magazine, I came across a rather unusual yet stirring poem on the subject of toughness and courage. The youth I have read it to have seemed very impressed; I've had excellent feedback from it:

THE LABORS OF THOR[2]

Stiff as the icicles in their beards, the Ice Kings
Sat in the great cold hall and stared at Thor
Who had lumbered this far north to stagger them
With his gifts, which (back at home) seemed scarcely human.

---

[2]From *Sleeping in the Woods*, by David Wagoner. Copyright © 1974 by Indiana University Press. Reprinted by permission of the publisher. (Originally appeared in *The New Yorker*.)

"Immodesty forbids," his sideman Loki
Proclaimed throughout the preliminary bragging,
And reeled off Thor's accomplishments, fit for Sagas
Or a seat on the bench of the gods. With a sliver of beard

An Ice King picked his teeth: "Is he a drinker?"
And Loki boasted of challengers laid out
As cold as pickled herring. The Ice King offered
A horn-cup, long as a harp's neck, full of mead.

Thor braced himself for elbow and belly room
And tipped the cup and drank as deep as mackerel,
Then deeper, reaching down for the halibut
Till his broad belt buckled. He had quaffed one inch.

"Maybe he's better at something else," an Ice King
Muttered, yawning. Remembering the boulders
He'd seen Thor heave and toss in the pitch of anger,
Loki proposed a bout of lifting weights.

"You men have been humping rocks from here to there
For ages," an Ice King said. "They cut no ice.
Lift something harder." And he whistled out
A gray-green cat with cold, mouseholey eyes.

Thor gave it a pat, then thrust both heavy hands
Under it, stooped and heisted, heisted again,
Turned red in the face and bit his lip and heisted
From the bottom of his heart — and lifted one limp forepaw.

Now pink in the face himself, Loki said quickly
That heroes can have bad days, like bards and beggars,
But Thor of all mortals was the grossest wrestler
And would stake his demigodhood on one fall.

Seeming too bored to bother, an Ice King waved
His chilly fingers around the mead-hall, saying,
"Does anyone need some trifling exercise
Before we go glacier-calving in the morning?"

An old crone hobbled in, foul-faced and gamy,
As bent in the back as any [female] of burden,
As grey as water, as feeble as an oyster.
An Ice King said, "She's thrown some boys in her time."

Thor would have left, insulted, but Loki whispered,
"When word gets south, she'll be at least an ogress."
Thor reached out sullenly and grabbed her elbow,
But she quicksilvered him and grinned her gums.

Thor tried his patented hammerlock takedown,
But she melted away like steam from a leaky sauna.
He tried a whole Nelson; it shrank to half, to a quarter,
Then nothing. He stood there, panting at the ceiling,

"Who got me into this demigoddiness?"
As flashy as lightning, the woman belted him
With her bony fist and boomed him to one knee,
But fell to a knee herself, as pale as moonlight.

Bawling for shame, Thor left by the back door,
Refusing to be consoled by Loki's plans
For a quick revision of the Northodox Version
Of the evening deeds. . . .

He went back south, tasting his bitter lesson,
Moment by moment, for the rest of his life,
Believing himself a pushover faking greatness
Along a tawdry strain of misadventures.

Meanwhile, the Ice Kings trembled in their chairs
But not from the cold — they'd seen a man hoist high
The Great Horn-Cup that ends deep in the ocean
And lower all Seven Seas by his own stature;

They'd seen him budge the Cat of the World and heft
The pillar of one paw, the whole north corner;
They'd seen a mere man wrestle with Death herself
And match her knee for knee, grunting like thunder.

— David Wagoner

We learn a great lesson from "The Labors of Thor." Many of our exceptional young men do not understand their potential greatness. They see themselves as failures. We should help them to see their true image. When they find out who they really are — bishops, stake presidents, apostles, great political and business leaders and executives — they will gain a self-image that will stay with them. Like the Ice Kings, we would sometimes tremble in our chairs if we knew who we are destined to be.

But what of youth who have serious tragedies in their lives — the loss of an eye, an arm, or a leg, or maybe a lesser loss? To the young person involved, life often seems hopeless, and quietly they give up hope for the future. To such we need to supply images of perseverance. Many years ago I read an article entitled "I Owe My Career to Losing a Leg," by Major Alexander P. de Seversky. He tells how he lost a leg and the adjustments that took place in his life. His comments should be an inspiration to anyone who has suffered a handicap.[3]

> I discovered early that the hardest thing to overcome is not a physical disability but the mental condition which it induces. The world, I found, has a way of taking a man pretty much at his own rating. If he permits his loss to make him embarrassed and apologetic, he will draw embarrassment from others. But if he gains his own respect, the respect of those around him comes easily.
>
> After a while I was able to talk about my disability with as little self-consciousness as men do about encroaching baldness or any other unpleasant physical fact. The adjustment wasn't easy. Often my friends exhibited a well-meaning pity which I deeply resented. The basic piece of advice to the sound of limb, in dealing with those who are not, is to ignore the matter — not to avoid it or pretend not to notice, but to treat it as a circumstance of minor importance. In the sum total of a man's abilities and essential character, a leg more or less is quite incidental.
>
> Year by year I regained physical skills which I thought had been lost forever. Greater agility and power with my hands and arms became my reward for the loss of a leg. I adjusted myself to the knowledge that I could not move as quickly as others and that this put me at a disadvantage in some sports — tennis, for instance. But in golf, where control, balance and coordination are more important than speed, I could match other people.
>
> The job of relearning how to skate and do fancy figures was not easy; but the pride in achievement once the job was done more than made up for the effort. Swimming, curiously, is the easiest of physical exercises for a legless person. For a swimmer minus one leg, weight is reduced more than total displacement in the water and buoyancy is increased.
>
> The awareness that others were noticing my physical condition, on the beach or on the diving board, ceased to bother me. On the contrary — and that, too, is one of the marvels of human nature — I developed a kind of inner pride about it. It was as if I had with me always the symbol of my victory over difficulties.

---

[3]© 1944 by Downe Publishing, Inc. Reprinted by permission of *Ladies' Home Journal*. As condensed in the September 1944 *Reader's Digest*.

I first met Evelyn Olliphant, of New Orleans, on a "blind date" to which I was taken by a friend in the Air Corps. I fell in love with her. I took her flying, driving, swimming. Any shyness either of us might have felt about my condition was thoroughly dissipated as the sense of comradeship grew between us. She is now Mrs. Seversky. Strange though it may sound, I am convinced that the absent limb, if it affected Mrs. Seversky's attitude at all, served only to enhance her tenderness for me.

Today, I feel it a solemn obligation to help those who are newly handicapped. The best that I can do, usually, is to make them understand that life remains rich and exciting and fruitful despite a physical disability: that life has a wonderful, inscrutable way of "paying off" in other things for any physical limitations. I cannot resist the temptation to tell the fathers and mothers and sweethearts of our boys in the services that my own mother, who was in despair when I was wounded, lived long enough to recognize that my "handicap" was in many respects a blessing in disguise.

And how about the images of persistence? Someone said, "Press on — nothing in the world can take the place of persistence. Talent will not; nothing is more common than unsuccessful men with talent. Genius will not; unrewarded genius is almost a proverb. Education alone will not; the world is full of educated derelicts. Persistence and determination alone are omnipotent." We may well add to that, "with a spiritual balance and a dedication to keep the commandments of the Savior."

Because not all our young people respond in the same way, we have challenges that test us to the very limit as leaders, and here is where we need to display the images of love and forgiveness. Someone said, "There is no more effective way to restore or raise your ego than by being courteous in times of difficulty." We need to underline this point in working with youth; we need to repeat it over and over again, for I believe that the truly great and noble souls are those who have learned to be courteous under pressure. Those people have likewise learned to forgive.

President Harold B. Lee in a conference address once said, "I came to a night some years ago when upon my bed

I realized that before I could be worthy of the high place to which I had been called I must love and forgive every soul that walked the earth, and at that time *I came to know,* and I received a peace, and a direction, and a comfort, and an inspiration that told me [of] things to come and gave me impressions that I knew were from a divine source."

We as leaders ought to have the ability to love and forgive every soul that walks the earth. And of course those who will offend us most and hurt us the deepest are members of the Church. When we forgive someone, we should forget. How cruel to remember and to discuss a person's weaknesses or problems when he or she may well have repented and overcome those problems! The Master Teacher in his love would have us forgive and forget. Let our young people who stumble and make great mistakes be forgiven.

I am sorry to say that many young people who might become great have been told far too often by parents or others that the door to a mission is closed, the door to temple marriage is closed, court action will be taken, or forgiveness is out of the question. This is wrong. No parent or leader other than the common judges in Israel should ever make such a judgment.

Helen Field Fisher teaches this point in a verse:

THE NEW LEAF

He came to my desk with quivering lip —
    The lesson was done.
"Dear Teacher, I want a new leaf," he said,
    "I have spoiled this one."
I took the old leaf, stained and blotted,
And gave him a new one, all unspotted,
    And into his sad eyes smiled:
    "Do better now, my child!"

I went to the Throne with a quivering soul —
    The old year was done.
"Dear Father, hast Thou a new leaf for me?
    "I have spoiled this one."

> He took the old leaf, stained and blotted,
> And gave me a new one, all unspotted,
> And into my sad heart smiled:
> "Do better now, my child!"

The bishop is the common judge in Israel. He will determine judgments and actions to be taken in the case of serious sin. The rest of us have a responsibility to close the matter in our minds and leave it with the bishop.

Anyone who has served as a bishop, a stake president, a General Authority, or a mission president understands the miracle of forgiveness. He has seen lives transformed by it from spiritual darkness to enlightenment.

Youth leaders have seen young people move to become totally sweet and pure before the Lord and make great and noble contributions throughout their lives. In our teaching and training we should never forget this great principle of forgiveness. It should be taught often, and with power and conviction.

We come now to the image of self-importance. William James, a noted psychologist, said, "The deepest need in human nature is the craving to be appreciated." What an opportunity, what an organization, we have to provide this in the life of every Aaronic Priesthood holder and young woman in the Church! The Lord has so organized his program that every young man has a peer leader — a deacons quorum president, a teachers quorum president, an assistant to the president of the priests quorum. Every young woman has a class president. These peer leaders are backed up in turn by fine leaders who have been raised up for the very purpose of preparing a generation of youth that will be the means of blessing the world.

As leaders, it is our responsibility to form images of self-importance in the minds of our youth. We ought to write letters to every single young person who achieves in any way. A simple note or card from an Aaronic Priesthood or Young Women's leader is so appreciated, so important. A special letter signed by all three members of the bishopric would be appropriate and undoubtedly be put in a book of remembrance. A stake president may, with his counselors, sign a special letter of commendation, appreciation or congratulations for any achievement or special activity of any young person that may come to his attention. Young people need to be appreciated — they need to *picture themselves* as being appreciated for a job well done.

Let me share some thoughts on what I think of as images of purity. They come from a book that has impressed me more than any other I have ever read with the exception of the scriptures — *Les Miserables* by Victor Hugo. The copy I have is 1220 pages long. The first time I read it I decided I would need to read forty pages a night for thirty days to finish it. I kept this promise to myself; however, one Saturday night as I neared the end with approximately 250 pages to go I started reading at about eleven o'clock. At 2:30 in the morning I finally laid the book down, having finished it, tears streaming down my cheeks for having had one of the greatest spiritual experiences of my life.

Vicariously I had associated with one of the great and noble men portrayed in this beautiful classic, Jean Valjean. If you are a leader of girls you may wish to consider this passage as appropriate for a very special evening stressing purity and moral cleanliness:

> We may, in extreme cases, introduce the reader into a nuptial chamber, not into a maiden's chamber. Verse would hardly dare, prose ought not. It is the interior of a flower yet unblown, it is a whiteness in the shade, it is the inmost cell of a closed lily which ought not to be looked upon by man, while yet it has not been looked upon by the sun. Woman in the bud is sacred. The innocent bed which is thrown open, the adorable semi-nudity which is afraid of itself, the white foot which takes refuge in a slipper, the bosom which veils itself before a mirror as if that mirror were an eye; the chemise which hastens up to hide the shoulder at the snapping of a piece of furniture, or at the passing of a wagon, the ribbons tied, the clasps hooked, the lacings drawn, the starts, the shivers of cold and of modesty, the exquisite shyness in every movement, the almost winged anxiety where there is no cause for fear; the successive phases of the dress as charming as the clouds of the

dawn; it is not fitting that all this should be described, and it is too much, indeed, to refer to it.

The eye of man should be more religious still before the rising of a young maiden than before the rising of a star. The possibility of touch should increase respect. The down of peach, the dust of the plum, the radiated crystal of the snow, the butterfly's wing powdered with feathers, are gross things in presence of that chastity which does not even know that it is chaste. The young maiden is only the gleam of a dream, and is not yet statue. Her alcove is hidden in the shadows of the ideal. The indiscreet touch of the eye defaces this dim penumbra. Here, to gaze is to profane.

So often many of our young women become coarse, exposed to filth, dirty stories, vile language, immodest dress, and vulgar, uncouth young men. Such a passage as the above becomes an ideal for our young women — a strengthening agent against the temptations of impurity.

At the area conference in Sweden in 1974, President Spencer W. Kimball talked to the priesthood brethren. In that very special setting he talked about the potentiality of those great nations, Denmark, Finland, Norway and Sweden. He talked about the possibility of districts becoming stakes, of stakes being divided, and the eventuality of many stakes. He talked about the people living worthy and pure, having sufficient activity and interest and being willing financially to build holy temples in those beautiful Nordic countries.

As I had the privilege of being at that conference I watched the faces of the priesthood men as they shared the vision of the future with the prophet. This vision — this challenge — will someday be realized. And many of the ordinary young men in that conference, many of the ordinary mature leaders there, will become great and mighty leaders because of the image of promise left by the prophet in their minds.

There is greatness in all of us. We as adult leaders need to feel deeply that every living soul has the potential to become as God is. Our task is to help our youth to achieve greatness in this life — in whatever job they are called upon to do. Our responsibility is to assist this generation of young people to achieve a degree of excellence not known in the world and in the kingdom at this time. We need to love the youth with the pure love of Christ. We should understand that regardless of the obnoxious acts many of them commit — regardless of their unwillingness to cooperate or to accept responsibility in this day — eventually, as we continue to work with and train them, they will measure up and become the Lord's very highest and noblest leaders.

It would be well for you as a youth leader to write the names of the young persons over whom you have stewardship, write the special qualities that you think God gave to each of them, and then write each one a letter and remind them of these qualities. Remind them of the influence that they have with their peers — remind them of their potential and their destiny.

Then remind yourself of the ways in which you can inspire them to fulfill that destiny.

3
THE WORTH
OF WORK

The Lord expects us, with wholehearted effort, to inspire and motivate our youth to be industrious, to be mentally and physically ambitious.

"There ain't no such thing as a free lunch," I remember reading many years ago.

I could believe that. You see, I grew up in a home that was regularly visited by bill collectors. A steady income just wasn't in our scheme of things.

Many times my Uncle Ernest would go down to his employer, ask for a salary advance, and bring us money so that we could buy food. He worked extra hours, extra days, so that we could have enough to eat. Later, when my mother and father were divorced, my family received neither subsistence nor alimony. We simply made it on our own with the help of great men like Uncle Ernest. It's not difficult, then, to understand my anxiety on that special day of my first job. I was fifteen at the time.

I remember going to work in a food market, terrified that I might not be able to hold the job if I didn't really work, running back and forth to every assignment given me.

My mother had sat down with me before I went to work. She had told me I'd be expected to work a full, hard day for each day's wages — and believe me, wages in those days didn't really amount to much. So I worked. Hard.

I had been at the market only a short time when I heard my boss talking to one of the produce managers from a different store. "I believe I'd rather have Vaughn work for me than any man I know," he said. I'll never forget what that comment did for me — the security which that one short statement gave me, and the pride it gave my mother. I thought, as someone said, that "compliments aren't what we *are,* but what we *should* be." And I knew that if I had to drop in my tracks working, I would live up to the reputation my boss had given me.

It was my responsibility to go to work early — at 6:00 A.M. — to open up the store for the other department heads. Each day I would feel the need to get there a little earlier and put in a little more work, and I would get there at 5:45, then 5:30, then just a little after five. And I would often work later than normal.

I remember working many times all night to get the job done, then working through the next day — working hours weren't then controlled by federal law. I simply worked to do my job and to outstrip the other fellows who were trying to work their way up in the organization. I would try to work faster and longer — to do better quality work than anyone else. And with the foundation my mother instilled in me concerning work, I was able to move up very quickly in that company.

Many mornings when I went to work I felt the need to begin my day with prayer. I would go to the back of the store by the switch panel and kneel down before turning on the lights. I'd say a verbal prayer, then turn on the lights and commence my work with all the fury I could muster, retrimming and filling the produce rack.

One morning, after my prayer, I saw the general manager of the company walking out the other side of the store.

He had hidden himself in the back room where he could watch those of us who came in early, to see if we would steal food items and things from the drug side of the store such as radios, knives, wrenches, and whatever else might appeal to a young man. I wondered how he must have felt as he sat back there waiting and watching to see if I was dishonest, and then hearing a very personal prayer from a young man to his Heavenly Father, asking for the ability to work hard, to be diligent, to get the job done.

So far as I know, he never again came back to check on me.

I noticed in those years that many others — even store managers in some cases — would come in, stand by the magazine rack, putter around and waste ten or fifteen minutes. They'd go back to the bakery and eat a hot roll or have a cup of coffee, then they'd wander to the back of the store and slowly put on their aprons.

I was always dismayed at those who'd been able to gain promotions and advancement — men and women who still had not learned that when you're on the payroll you've been hired to give your maximum effort to the job.

And I was always glad I had the opportunity to find out the value of work at such an early age, and always grateful to my mother for "setting me straight" about work.

Not every young person, even in those days, started a career with that advantage. Today the question is, At a time when our young men and women tend to look fondly to the "easy life," when they want more and more time off, when they see their peers getting by with as little effort as possible, how do we teach the value of a good day's work?

Truly as parents and leaders of youth we are in the attitude-changing business. We are to teach youth that work is not only honorable but is the essence of progression. As President J. Reuben Clark, Jr., puts it, "We must purge our hearts of the love of ease; we must put from our lives the curse of idleness." I might add that President Clark himself was a master worker. He worked long, diligent hours at the office. After going home he would have dinner and maybe relax for a short time, then he'd work again at his desk long into the night — studying, thinking, and preparing works that would assist the Church in accomplishing its great mission.

The whole attitude of work that we are focusing on is summed up in a quaint but meaningful little poem titled "The Little Red Hen." It's worth reading to your youth:

THE LITTLE RED HEN

Said the big white rooster, "Gosh all hemlock; things are really tough,
Seems that worms are getting scarcer and I cannot find enough;
What's become of all those fat ones is a mystery to me;
There were thousands through the rosy spell but now where can they
    be?"

The little red hen who heard him didn't grumble or complain,
She had gone through lots of dry spells, she had lived through floods of
    rain;
So she flew up on the grindstone and she gave her claws a whet,
As she said: "I've never seen the time there were no worms to get."

She picked a new and undug spot — the earth was hard and firm,
The big white rooster jeered, "New ground! That's no place for a worm."
The little red hen just spread her feet, she dug both fast and free,
"I must go to the worms," she said, "the worms won't come to me."

The rooster vainly spent his day, through habit, by the ways
Where fat worms have passed in squads, back in the rainy days.
When nightfall found him supperless, he growled in accents rough,
"I'm hungry as a fowl can be — conditions sure are tough."

He turned then to the little red hen and said, "It's worse with you,
For you're not only hungry but you must be tired, too.
I rested while I watched for worms, so I feel fairly perk,
But how are you? Without worms, too? And after all that work?"

The little red hen hopped to her perch and dropped her eyes to sleep,
And murmured in a drowsy tone, "Young man, hear this and weep.
I'm full of worms and happy, for I've dined both long and well.
The worms are there as always — but I had to dig like H- - - !"

Oh, here and there, white roosters still are holding sales positions,
They cannot do much business now, because of poor conditions,
But as soon as things get right again, they'll sell a hundred firms —
Meanwhile the little red hens are out a-gobbling up the worms.

— Author unidentified

As we approach the awesome task of instilling the honor,
the *rightness* of work in our youth, we can set our sights on
three totally reliable, totally practical guidelines. Here they
are:

We should teach by precept and by example. As Walt
Whitman so effectively said in an earlier age of uncertainty,
"He that speaks to me in the right voice, him will I follow
as I follow the moon . . . anywhere about the globe." In
other words, youth watch what we do. They imitate us — for
better or for worse.

Youth are best taught at home. The Church has some
splendid youth programs, programs of enormous value to the
youth and to parents who are looking for solid reinforcement.
But by far the greatest influence in teaching youth to be
ambitious, dedicated, persistent, work oriented, is *the home.*
Our job as youth leaders begins then at home, with our own
children.

Work can be exciting, uplifting. We need to teach our
youth not only that work is honorable but that it can be exciting, tremendously satisfying, even fun. Let's remember
how Tom Sawyer's friends paid him for the privilege of
whitewashing the fence. Tom had simply helped his friends
to find new appeal in an old job. And so can we!

Earlier in this chapter I indicated that my first real
work-for-pay experience began in the produce department of
a market. Years later, when I was a produce buyer for a
large grocery chain, conditions had changed and I was in the
position of judging the performance of those working under
me. I remember a particular weekend when I had bought
a large quantity of apples to support a weekend special we
were advertising throughout the state. As the Friday ad hit

the newsstands there was a tremendous run on the apples. In just a few hours we knew we'd be needing a lot more the next day — far more than we had expected.

I phoned the man who had sold us the apples, but got his forty-two-year-old son instead. I told him of our need. The son replied that in order to fill the order they would have to work all night long. Unbeknown to me, his father, sixty-eight at the time, was on the phone's extension. He piped in, saying, "Vaughn, you'll have the apples. We'll work all night and have them to your stores in the morning."

What a great example this veteran of hard work and striving taught his son — and taught me — that day and again on Saturday morning when all the apples were promptly delivered to our stores! The example was helpful in two ways: first, as a produce buyer I knew whom we could rely on for apples when we needed them; and second, as a father I came to realize how powerfully a man can set an example in the lives of his children.

I know a father who once felt the need to set such an example in the mind of his son Richard, who at thirteen weighed in at 160 pounds. This is how that father tells the story:

> I took him out to our pasture and told him we needed to dig a hole about four feet deep. We thrust in our shovels, the mid-morning sun hot against our backs. After the first thin layer of dirt, the remainder seemed like concrete as we worked together.
>
> I turned the project over to Rick while I did something else (so that I could watch him). He worked fairly well on his own — just *fairly* well. After a while I went out and joined him. I set out with the speed that I'd had in former years. I dug furiously, lifting heavy, full loads of dirt out of the hole. The perspiration rolled off my arms as our efforts gradually assumed the status of a real hole.
>
> Before long he volunteered to take a turn. I obligingly jumped out of the hole and then I watched him work. Now *he* worked with the same fierce pace he had seen me use, the sweat pouring down his face. The more I complimented him, the harder he worked — far into the hot afternoon. Finally the project was

completed, displaying its neatly trimmed sides and its impressive depth in the nearly impenetrable earth.

I remember that we had to come up with some *use* for the hole, so we took rocks from all over the field and threw them in. Then we covered them with the soft soil we'd dug out.

A make-work project, to be sure, but Richard learned a lesson that day. He learned how to really work when you have to, to take pride in a job done with energy and enthusiasm — even if it's just digging a hole with Dad.

There's no finer example of building pride into your work than in the story "The Countess and the Impossible," by Richard Thurman, a story that shows our youth there's always a little more they can put into any job.

THE COUNTESS AND THE IMPOSSIBLE[1]

No one in our small Utah town knew where the Countess had come from; her carefully precise English indicated that she was not a native American. From the size of her house and staff we knew that she must be wealthy, but she never entertained, and she made it clear that when she was at home she was completely inaccessible. Only when she stepped outdoors did she become at all a public figure, and then chiefly to the small fry of the town, who lived in awe of her.

The Countess always carried a cane, not only for support, but as a means of chastising any youngster she thought needed disciplining. And at one time or another most of the youngsters in our neighborhood seemed to display that need. By running fast and staying alert, I had managed to keep out of her reach. But one day when I was about thirteen, as I was short-cutting through her hedge, she got close enough to rap my head with the stick.

"Ouch!" I yelled, jumping a couple of feet.

"Young man, I want to talk to you," she said. I was expecting a lecture on the evils of trespassing, but as she looked at me, half smiling, she seemed to change her mind.

"Don't you live in that green house with the yellow trees in the next block?"

[1]Reprinted with permission from the June 1958 *Reader's Digest*. Copyright 1958 by The Reader's Digest Assn., Inc.

"Yes, Ma'am."

"Good. I've lost my gardener. Be at my house Thursday morning at seven, and don't tell me you have something else to do. I've seen you slouching on Thursdays."

When the Countess gave an order, it was carried out. I didn't dare not come on Thursday. I went over the whole lawn three times with a mower before she was satisfied, and then she had me down on all fours looking for weeds until my knees were as green as the grass. She finally called me up to the porch.

"Well, young man, how much do you want for your day's work?"

"I don't know. Fifty cents maybe."

"Is that what you figure you're worth?"

"Yes'm. About that."

"Very well. Here's the fifty cents you say you're worth, and here's the dollar and a half that I earned for you by pushing you. Now I'm going to tell you something about how you and I are going to work together. There are as many ways of mowing a lawn as there are people, and they may be worth anywhere from a penny to five dollars. Let's say that a three-dollar job would be just about what you have done today, except that you would do it all by yourself. A four-dollar job would be so perfect that you'd have to be something of a fool to spend that much time on a lawn. A five-dollar lawn is — well, it's impossible, so we'll forget about that. Now then, each week I'm going to pay you according to your own evaluation of your work."

I left with my two dollars, richer than I remembered being in my whole life, and determined that I would get four dollars out of her the next week. But I failed to reach even the three-dollar mark. My will began to falter the second time around her yard.

"Two dollars again, eh? That kind of puts you right on the edge of being dismissed, young man."

"Yes'm, but I'll do better next week."

And somehow I did. The last time around the lawn I was exhausted, but I found I could spur myself on. In the exhilaration of that new feeling, I had no hesitation in asking the Countess for three dollars.

Each Thursday for the next four or five weeks, I varied between a three- and a three-and-a-half-dollar job. The more I became acquainted with her lawn, places where the ground was a little high or a little low, places where it needed to be clipped short or left long on the edges to make a more satisfying curve along the garden, the more I became aware of just what a four-dollar lawn would consist of. And each week I would resolve to do just that kind of a job. But by the time I had my three-dollar or three-and-a-half-dollar mark I was too tired to remember even having had the ambition to go beyond that.

"You look like a good consistent three-dollar-and-fifty-cent man," she would say as she handed me the money.

"I guess so," I would say, too happy at the sight of the money to remember that I had shot for something higher.

"Well, don't feel too bad," she would comfort me. "After all, there are only a handful of people in the world who could do a four-dollar job."

And her words *were* a comfort at first, but then, without my noticing what was happening, her comfort became an irritant that made me resolve to do that four-dollar job, even if it killed me. In the fever of my resolve, I could see myself expiring on her lawn, with the Countess leaning over me, handing me the four dollars with a tear in her eye, begging my forgiveness for having thought I couldn't do it.

It was in the middle of such a fever, one Thursday night when I was trying to forget the day's defeat and get some sleep, that the truth hit me so hard that I sat upright, half choking in my excitement. It was the *five-dollar* job I had to do, not the four-dollar one. I had to do the job that no one could do because it was impossible.

I was well acquainted with the difficulties ahead. I had the problem, for example, of doing something about the worm mounds in the lawn. The Countess might not even have noticed them yet, they were so small; but in my bare feet I knew about them and I had to do something about them. And I could go on trimming the garden edges with shears, but I knew that a five-dollar lawn demanded that I line up each edge exactly with a yardstick and then trim it precisely with the edger. And there were other problems that only I and my bare feet knew about.

I started the next Thursday by ironing out the worm mounds with a heavy roller. After two hours of that I was ready to give up for the day. Nine o'clock in the morning, and my will was already gone! It was only by accident that I discovered how to regain it. Sitting under a walnut tree for a few minutes after finishing the rolling, I fell asleep. When I woke up minutes later, the lawn looked so good and felt so good under my feet, I was anxious to get on with the job.

I followed this renewal secret for the rest of the day, dozing for a few minutes every hour to regain my perspective and replenish my strength. Between naps, I mowed four times, twice lengthwise and twice across, until the lawn looked like a green velvet checkerboard. Then I dug around every tree, crumbling the big clods and smoothing the soil with my hands, then finished with the edger, meticulously lining up each stroke so the effect would be perfectly symmetrical. And I carefully trimmed the grass between the flagstones of the front walk. The shears wore my fingers raw, but the walk never looked better.

Finally about eight o'clock that evening . . . it was all completed. I was so proud I didn't even feel tired when I went up to her door.

"Well, what is it today?" she asked.

"Five dollars," I said, trying for a little calm and sophistication.

"Five dollars? You mean four dollars, don't you? I told you that a five-dollar lawn job isn't possible."

"Yes it is. I just did it."

"Well, young man, the first five-dollar lawn in history certainly deserves some looking around."

We walked about the lawn together in the light of evening, and even I was quite overcome by the impossibility of what I had done.

"Young man," she said, putting her hand on my shoulder, "what on earth made you do such a crazy, wonderful thing?"

I didn't know why, but even if I had, I could not have explained it in the excitement of hearing that I had done it.

"I think I know," she continued, "how you felt when this idea came to you of caring for a lawn that I told you was impossible. It made you very happy when it first came, then a little frightened. Am I right?"

She could see she was right by the startled look on my face.

"I know how you felt, because the same thing happens to almost everyone. They feel this sudden burst in them of wanting to do some great thing. They feel a wonderful happiness, but then it passes because they have said, 'No, I can't do that. It's impossible.' Whenever something in you says, 'It's impossible,' remember to take a careful look and see if it isn't really God asking you to grow an inch, or a foot, or a mile, that you may come to a fuller life."

Since that time, some twenty-five years ago, when I have felt myself at an end with nothing before me, suddenly, with the appearance of that word "impossible," I have experienced the unexpected lift, the leap inside me, and known that the only possible way lay through the very middle of impossible.

We may not know exactly where the boy received all the push to go for the five-dollar job; quite possibly the Countess simply drove home a lesson that had first been taught at home. But this we know for certain: Fathers and mothers have the first responsibility to teach boys and girls how to work. As leaders of youth, we can step in as the Countess did, doing all we can to confirm the teachings at home. And in those cases where little or nothing is taught at home, we should do everything we can to fill the breach and help prepare these young people for the work that lies ahead — for missions, for successful vocations and professions, for happy homes.

But let's never forget that ideally the whole process of teaching the value of work really begins with us at home, teaching our own children first.

Suppose our youth come to us and say, "Come on, now, work can't be all *that* great!" What then?

Give them some alternatives. Show them how they can use their free agency to do absolutely *nothing* if they please. And then show them what kind of rewards they can expect to reap for that kind of effort. Here are some examples that will help you.

At a meeting I attended in Los Angeles, a corporation president addressing the meeting told this story:

Four hundred years ago a Japanese gardener planted a small pine tree in one inch of soil in a shallow dish. He trimmed each root and branch as the tree grew. When he died, his son took up the task, and so on down through nineteen generations. Today that tree stands, never having outgrown the original dish, in the Kuhura Gardens in Tokyo. After four hundred years, it is only twenty inches high with a twisted top some thirty-six inches across. Though growing all these many years, because of its management it is exactly where it began.

Environmental or climatic conditions could have also dwarfed the tree's expansion.

Here is another quotation (whose authorship I cannot identify) which you might use on someone who needs steering away from the "soft job" philosophy.

> The writer/clergyman Henry Ward Beecher was once asked by a young man where he might find a job that paid well and involved no hard work.
>
> "Young man, you cannot be an editor," replied Beecher. "Do not try the law. Do not think of the ministry. Do not think of manufacturing and merchandising. Abhor politics. Don't practice medicine. Don't be a farmer or a soldier or a sailor. All those require too much study and thinking. My son, you have come into a hard, hard world. There is only one easy place in it, and that is the grave."
>
> Possibly the biggest handicap a young man can have is to land a soft job early in his career. He loses the opportunity of learning that the only kind of soft job worth having is one that he himself has softened up by a lot of hard work.
>
> A young person should look at the trees that stand out in the open, buffeted by the winds, and compare them with the spindling ones which have been so protected that it wasn't necessary for them to send their roots deep down into the soil to get a stronger hold and more nourishment.
>
> The fortunate man today is the one who has a reasonably hard job and the ability and willingness to handle it. Soft jobs make soft men. Don't waste envy on the fellow with a soft job.

In a similar vein, an ad for Marstellar Inc. appearing in the *Wall Street Journal* tells how easy it is to retire at thirty-five:

> It's easy.
>
> Thousands of men do it every year. In all walks of life.
>
> And it sets our economy, our country, and the world back thousands of years in terms of wasted human resources. But worst of all is the personal tragedy that almost always results from "early retirement."

It usually begins with a tinge of boredom. Gradually a man's work begins to seem endlessly repetitious. The rat race hardly seems worth it any more. It's at this point that many a thirty-five-year-old boy-wonder retires. There are no testimonial dinners or gold watches. He still goes to work every day, puts in his forty hours, and even draws a paycheck. He's retired, but nobody knows it. Not at first, anyhow.

The lucky ones get fired in time to make a fresh start. Those less fortunate hang on for awhile — even decades — waiting and wondering. Waiting for a raise or promotion that never comes; and wondering why.

There are ways to fight back, though, and most men do. They counteract the urge to coast by running as they've never run before. They run until they get the second wind that is now known as "self-renewal."

Self-renewal is nothing more or less than doing for yourself what your parents, teachers, coaches, and bosses did for you when you seemed young enough to need it. It's the highest form of self-discipline. And it can be one of the most satisfying experiences a man can enjoy.

Self-renewal is the adult's ability to motivate himself; to reawaken his self-pride in the face of spiritual fatigue.

Self-renewal is the device by which the boy-wonders become men. Leaders. Creators. Thinkers.

Self-renewal is probably the greatest test a businessman must face. It's worth the effort, though. With the life expectancy approaching the century mark, sixty-five years is a long time to spend in a rocking chair.

Throughout my life I have believed — and now I understand even more firmly than ever — that soft jobs make soft men. By *soft* I am talking about easy jobs — jobs that require as little as possible and pay as much as possible.

Let's be realistic: In most cases, today's business will pay for the man who can get at the job, do it, and then go on to the next one. We need to have a glory about the work we do, and that glory comes from wrapping up the job, achieving the result. In this day bosses pay for *results,* not for excuses. Lynn Fluckinger says it in his book *Dynamic Leadership:* "No matter how good or how valid, the excuse never changes performance." Ralph Waldo Emerson puts it another way: "What you would have — pay the price and take it."

Work, of course, has its applications throughout life — and presumably throughout eternity — for one simple reason: It is the key to learning, to growth, to eternal progression. And nowhere, perhaps, is the need for work more sharply focused than upon missionaries in The Church of Jesus Christ of Latter-day Saints.

One of the great crying concerns by our mission presidents across the Church is that missionaries have not learned how to work. They don't know what it is to get up at 6:30 in the morning and study and then do their housework. They don't know how to go out and tract for hours on end. They don't know how to come home in the afternoon or evening, have dinner quickly, go back out and teach through the early evening hours, and then have the self-discipline to be in bed on time — in short, to follow the missionary schedule.

Clearly we need to prepare these young men for the sacred trust they will have for the two years they are on their mission, and for the responsibilities they are sure to have with the Church, their families and their jobs following their mission service.

As youth leaders who have daily contact with the young men who will join the thousands of missionaries now in the field, we might well remind them that in the final analysis their success will derive not from their parents, nor from the Church, nor from their mission presidents, nor from their companions, nor from their districts. That success will spring directly from what they put into their work. As is suggested in this poem, it comes right back to "the man in the glass":

THE MAN IN THE GLASS

When you get what you want in your struggle for self,
And the world makes you king for a day,
Just go to the mirror and look at yourself,
And see what that man has to say.

For it isn't your father or mother or wife
    Whose judgment upon you must pass.
The fellow whose verdict counts most in your life,
    Is the one staring back from the glass.

You may be like Jack Horner and chisel a plum
    And think you're a wonderful guy,
But the man in the glass, he says you're a bum
    If you can't look him straight in the eye.

He's the fellow to please, never mind all the rest,
    For he's with you clear to the end,
And you've passed your most dangerous, difficult test
    If the man in the glass is your friend.

You may fool the whole world down the pathway of years
    And get pats on the back as you pass.
But your final reward will be heartache and tears,
    If you've cheated the man in the glass.

                    — Author unidentified

Someone has said, "No missionary is ever greater the rest of his life than while he was on his mission." In other words, if as a missionary he or she truly works hard, is successful, achieves results, has the ability to use ambition and focus it wisely, later in life success will follow in other fields too.

But what happens when the going gets rough? In missionary work, in homemaking, in any kind of job, our youth will encounter situations which may seem beyond them: criticism, failure to achieve a desired result, interference, poor health — these can build up or combine to produce some difficult, desperate feelings.

We might well remember the blistered hands of the boy with the grass clippers in "The Countess and the Impossible"; or the hard-as-concrete sandstone that Richard dug through on a summer day; or my own fear that I might lose my first job, and with it the income my family needed. After all, the going *does* get rough. We should remember that Heavenly Father has never signed a contract with anyone promising him a life of pure ease and happiness.

Annie Johnson Flint put it this way in a poem:

PROMISES

God hath not promised
Skies always blue,
Flower-strewn pathways
All our lives through;
God hath not promised
Sun without rain,
Joy without sorrow,
Peace without pain.

But God hath promised
Strength for the day,
Rest for the labor,
Light for the way,
Grace for the trials,
Help from above,
Unfailing sympathy,
Undying love.

Discouragement, despair, desperation have their common synonym in the Lord's scheme of things: opposition. It's there for a purpose. It's there to be experienced, to be benefited from as each obstacle is surmounted. As parents and leaders of youth, we would be just as remiss in shielding them from their problems as would the Lord be in withholding from us deserved blessings.

The concept of work may have been easier to teach a century or so ago when the going was tougher. Or was it? As I think about that, I begin to realize that our youth today are facing new kinds of problems we never dreamed of at their age: the boredom of affluence and with it a shortage of hard-work situations; mothers away at work; the general availability of drugs; widespread sexual promiscuity; environmental pollution; global unrest.

The opposition these days is packaged in a different wrap, but the chances to overcome opposition, to meet challenges, to face realities, are still here for our youth. We ought to write the word *work* in four-inch block letters on our minds and on the minds of our youth. In work is to be found the most practical, meaningful solution to our problems, as this poem suggests:

IF YOU WANT A THING BAD ENOUGH

If you want a thing bad enough
To go out and fight for it,
Work day and night for it,
Give up your time and your peace and your sleep for it,
If only a desire of it
Makes your arm strong enough
Never to tire of it,
Makes you hold all things tawdry and cheap for it,
If life seems empty and useless without it
And all that you scheme and you dream is about it,
If gladly you sweat for it,
Fret for it,
Plan for it,
Lose all your terror of God and of man for it,
If you'll simply go after the thing that you want,
With all your capacity,
Strength and sagacity,
Faith, hope and confidence, stern pertinacity,
If neither cold, poverty, famished and gaunt,
Nor sickness, nor pain,
Of body and brain,
Can turn you away from the thing that you want,
If dogged and grim you besiege and beset it,
YOU'LL GET IT!

— Author unidentified

As parents and youth leaders we must reach out — our people must reach out. We need to share with the whole world our attitudes about work, about God, country, loyalty, patriotism. We ought to share those values we hold most dear, for in them we find the real keys to happiness, to success, to eternal progression.

It is a marvelous thing for the spirit, for the personality, for the character and integrity of man to learn the value of hard work — and it is equally important to be able to *teach* its value. Our young people who catch the vision of work will provide the greatest leadership for the Church, for organizations, corporations, and governmental offices, of any generation in history. Consequently we should inspire and motivate them. We should help to make them the most highly motivated generation of youth in history. The times require it.

As Church members, wherever we find ourselves we ought to make our standards of work and living an example for all nations. For as the Savior said, we need to set our light upon a hill and not under a bushel. And as we do this, ours will be the great joy of seeing the next generation outstrip us in their ability to work.

Most significantly, we need to induce in our youth the understanding that work is a privilege and a blessing — one which is to be part of every young man and woman who would aspire to godhood.

4
COMMUNICATING WITH YOUTH

The real message they receive is not the one they hear from our lips. It is the spirit-to-spirit, soul-to-soul message that our innermost feelings convey — for better or worse.

"You don't really care about me, do you?"

"I'm just somebody to *do things* for you, aren't I?"

"Do you love me?"

Perhaps you've heard the questions directly from your teen-agers. Or perhaps you've *felt* them, coming in loud and clear as *unspoken* communications. In either case, what a tragedy it is when our youth question our basic motives as parents, question our love — especially in that majority of cases where, for some reason, we have simply failed to communicate as parents!

Well, as mothers, fathers and youth leaders we are largely to blame.

For one thing, we criticize, complain about and degrade our youth in a one-way stream of negative messages. We criticize them for not being on time; for playing their stereo too loudly or on the wrong station; for being on the telephone too long, in the bathroom too long; for squeezing the toothpaste in the middle; for wearing their hair too long; for wearing the wrong clothes. Then we turn around sweetly and send them on an endless number of errands and jobs that fit neatly into *our* scheme of things, but seemingly without consideration of their time schedules.

We seem to do very well at *sending* messages of annoyance or requests for help, but where are we, as *receivers,* when our youth urgently need us to listen? The problem is so general that we have developed handy terms like "communications gap" and "generation gap" to describe it — as though it were an inevitable consequence of twentieth-century living.

The question of whether or not we are communicating — that is, freely exchanging thoughts on a continuous, two-way basis — inevitably leads away from our homes and into our stewardships in leading youth. Are we really communicating with our youth in Sunday School? in priesthood meeting? in Scouts? Or is it the same old one-way message beaming endlessly out from our lips to a listless, turned-off group of teen-agers?

The idea that *we communicate what we feel* has intrigued me for years; it suggests that the key to good communication is not necessarily in being able to form words or fashion an eloquent speech, but rather in effectively transmitting our innermost attitudes to those around us. If this be so, we should begin — each of us — with our own personal attitudes: our attitudes about ourselves, about life, about the Church, about the youth with whom we've been called to work as parents or youth leaders.

I can't think of a better example of how attitudes affect feelings, and how feelings form communications, than one involving my son Scott when he was twelve.

Our stake had planned a full-blown, two-day track and sports meet, complete with all sorts of races, cross-country, field events, basketball shooting, sit-ups, chin-ups, and a number of other events — the whole works. Six weeks before the meet, Scott had taken a crash on a motorcycle (it was his first time aboard), and with forty-two stitches across his knee he wasn't in the best shape for running. But just four days after the doctor took the bandages off, Scott, correctly thinking that his leg would prevent him from entering the sprints, ran the cross-country and finished in second place. Of course we were proud to think that Scott, in spite of this condition, had the heart to keep on going.

The next day he was very concerned; he couldn't think of anything he could enter in which he could score some points.

I said to him, "Well, enter anything that you and the ward can get some points for. Even if you take last place you can participate and still be a good sport."

Scott got involved in the sit-up event, and the next thing I knew his mother came over to me and said, "I want you to go over and stop the boy. He's done over five hundred sit-ups!"

"No," I said, "I'm not going to stop him, and don't you stop him either. Let him keep going; he knows what it takes to be someone. You let him go."

A short time later she came back and said "Vaughn, I want you to stop the boy. He's done seven hundred and fifty sit-ups and I want you to *stop* him. His back is bleeding. Please get him to stop."

"No, Merlene," I replied. "If you can't stand the sight of blood, stay here and walk around with me, but don't stop Scott. He'll know when to stop."

So a while later, over Scott came, a big grin across his face and a blue ribbon in his hand.

"How did you do, Scott?" I asked.

"I took first place."

"How many sit-ups?"

"I did one thousand and one."

You can imagine how proud we were that afternoon. But as I look back I see some tremendously powerful communication having taken place: communication between a determined young man driving toward a higher self-worth in the face of an injury handicap; a concerned, protective mother asserting her rightful role in watching out for her son; a father, feeling his son's need to be someone, to have a sense of worth, to begin cutting the apron strings.

The feelings were all there, playing powerfully as Scott won the blue ribbon. And the feelings were intensified the next day in church when the bishop announced Scott's name along with the other achievers.

No communications barriers remained that day. A feeling of pride pervaded the family, bringing our preteen-age son one more step along in his self-esteem and one important step closer to his bishop, who had recognized him publicly.

Actually my wife Merlene communicates excellently with youth. She has had amazing success in working with young women; they fall deeply in love with her. They come to the house and discuss their deepest concerns. It doesn't seem to matter whether they are active or inactive in the Church, or whether they are walking the fine line between major transgression and full activity in the Church — they still seem to find in her someone with whom they can communicate.

In our family we have five older sons, then a little girl, and then another son. My wife has the great ability to communicate with these beautiful souls and help their spirits.

Hers is a very special blessing. To this day she gets letters from those she worked with as the president of the MIA in a ward in Salt Lake City, another ward in Boise, and even further back — from women who themselves are now mothers.

As I have tried to analyze her great skill as a communicator, it seems to me that Merlene has the great ability to accept people for their own worth and to love them, to care about them and their problems. But always she's firm; she does not compromise or bend the principles of the gospel. I believe they respect her for this.

While we are concerned about communicating in Church situations, repeatedly we emphasize that communication begins in the home.

The home, with the father as patriarch and the mother in her strong supporting role, is where the highest level of teaching should take place, where the highest degree of communication should occur.

It follows that, as youth leaders charged with the awesome task of communicating the gospel, we should practice the fine art of communication, knitting a tight, eternal bond of regard between husband and wife, between parents and children, among sons and daughters. We ought to do nothing that would damage or destroy those "links of feeling" — those communications of love and understanding that are nurtured in our homes and blossom in our ward, branch, and stake youth leadership callings.

Whether we like it or not, the fine art of communication, whether at home or elsewhere, often requires time — and effort.

I have a son who as a boy almost worshipped basketball. When he was eleven, I had seen Dave clear the snow off the sidewalk on many a winter's evening and practice until ten-thirty or eleven at night. He'd come in with his hands blue from the cold, yet with that undaunted spirit he'd go out the next night and do the same thing again. By the time he was thirteen he could beat his father most of the time.

One hot August afternoon — I believe the temperature was about eighty-six degrees — I was out playing with him. We'd played hard and hot for about forty-five minutes, and I finally said, "Dave, I've had it. I'm going in and soak my head under some cold water and then lie down for a while."

I turned to leave, when he said, "Hey, Dad, remember that family championship we had last March?"

"Yes," I replied.

"You remember who the family champ was, don't you?"

I said, "Yes, you're the family champ."

"Well, how would you like to win that championship back today?"

I said, "No, Dave, not today. But I'll play another time." And I turned to walk into the house.

He called, "Chicken, huh?"

Well, I couldn't take that, so I went into the house, quickly soaked my head under the cold tap, and came back out. We started playing a game of twenty-two. Now, when you haven't played — as we hadn't — through the summer, neither of us was hitting many baskets.

We put a lot of pressure on each other — after all, a family championship was at stake — and in half an hour I was so exhausted I thought I'd die.

I remember that the score was eighteen to sixteen, and I thought, "If Dave can make two more baskets, the game will be over." (As you know, in a game of twenty-two you have to win by two baskets.)

I took the ball — it was my turn — and I thought, "Well, before this game ends I'd better teach him a lesson." So I laid the ball on my hip and I said, "Dave, you just remember this." And I recited a verse called "The Champion."

> The average runner runs until the breath in him is gone,
> But the champion has the iron will that makes him carry on.
> For rest the average runner begs when limp his muscles grow,
> But the champion runs on leaden legs, his courage makes him go.
> The average man's complacent when he's done his best to score,
> But the champion does his best, and then he does a little more.

Well, Dave looked at me and his eyes got big. He couldn't believe what he was hearing his dad say. But that wasn't the amazing thing. The amazing thing that happened was deep inside me; I felt a welling of strength that I didn't know existed, and I knew I could meet the test.

We played on and pretty soon it was twenty-two to twenty-four, then twenty-six to twenty-four, then twenty-eight to twenty-six. Then Dave took the ball out of bounds and he laid it on his hip and said, "Dad, the man who won't be beaten, *can't* be beaten."

Well, that just about did it. But we played on and pretty soon the score ended thirty-eight to thirty-four. Who won? That depends on who tells the story.

What was *really* important that afternoon was that communication was going on. Dave was communicating what kind of a boy he was. I was communicating what kind of a dad I was. The feelings between father and son were flowing freely on that hot afternoon.

This kind of communication can take place in almost any situation in which parents and leaders are willing to devote a little time, a little effort, a little interest, a little love.

Basketball games are not the only effective vehicles for improving communication. Some adults seem always to communicate effectively. Others turn off their children, or their communication between parent or youth leader and teen-ager just seems to dry up. It's as though the teen-ager was inside a giant box with a little one-inch blind for convenient turning off. All they have to do, when they get turned off, is to pull down the little blind. They remain inside the box all right, but there is no communication.

The process happens every day, but there are solutions. Some years ago, when my oldest son was about fourteen, I seemed to be losing touch with him. I did not want this to happen, so I took him on a trip with me to Denver, Cheyenne, and back to Salt Lake City.

I did most of the talking the first two or three days, but finally on the third day my son began to loosen up. We began to talk about all sorts of things on a one-to-one basis, and our relationship began returning to normal. When we arrived home I decided I'd never again need to take two days to relearn how to communicate with my son. I resolved that the problem was mine, not his, and I would never stop working at correcting it.

I should say here, however, that it wouldn't have mattered if it had taken a week, a month, ten years, or fifty years to regain contact if that much time had been necessary. We should never stop trying, even when communication seems permanently lost.

Frequently there's a special, magical time for breaking down communication barriers. It's often (but not always) a father-to-son time, a mother-to-daughter time. And it's a late-hour time.

My wife has a very special talent for late-hour communication. Often our children will go to her to talk about things they'd never discuss with me. She'll sit up with them until eleven or twelve o'clock if necessary and talk through a problem. Then the next day she will come to me and say, "Did you know your son (or daughter) was feeling this way?" And I'll ask, "Why didn't he (or she) talk with me?"

"Well," Merlene answers, "you didn't take the time to sit down and talk it over." So she helps me to communicate. The great concern in our family is that the Lord will bless us to have at least one of us always communicating fully, so that there will be no problem with our family relationships.

We received a tape from our second oldest son while he was in the mission field. It came just before Christmas. Part of the tape he dedicated to his little sister, a part to each of his brothers, a part to his mother and then finally, at the end of the tape, was his message to me.

He talked at first about all of the basketball games I had watched him play. He wanted me to know how grateful he was that I had been there. He said, "I'm sure you think that was probably the most important thing you did for me, being there, supporting me."

Then he said: "You know what I dream about out here, what I long for? I want to spend some time with you. Remember the nights when you would come home tired from your stake president's meeting? It would be eleven or maybe midnight and I would have a problem, and I would say, 'Hey, Dad, let's go up on the top of the hill and talk.' I know now you must have been really tired, and we would walk up to the hill where we could sit and look out over Boise and see the lights. And then we would talk for forty-five minutes or an hour [mostly about his brother Ron in the mission field] and then come back down and go to bed."

He added, "Just to have a talk with you — that's what I miss most."

I pledged after hearing that tape I would try to make more time to spend with my younger sons, and that after Dave got home I would try to spend time with him again, if that's what he really wanted. And I believe it was.

If home life provides plenty of communications opportunities, certainly also do our youth leadership positions in church. In fact, two of the most spiritual experiences I ever had came about through the influence of great youth leaders at church.

I remember as a young man I had a great Scoutmaster, Buford Reynolds. I had received my tenderfoot and immediately began working on my second class. But I was obnoxious. One day after I had been in Scouts about a year, the Scoutmaster came to me and said, "Vaughn, you know, you have a great deal of talent and we could use you in leadership positions in the Church. But not when you act the way you do at troop meeting."

I believe that was the night I turned the corner. I think I got the message. But so did Brother Reynolds. He knew I wanted to be somebody. He knew I was trying to get attention, and he thought I should get it the *proper* way. So he prepared me, and a short time later I was called to be a patrol leader, and then senior patrol leader. From there I went on to gain my Eagle Scout rank, and since then I've had the privilege of working in Scouting for many years.

I look back on Brother Reynolds as one of the choice

men in my life — a man who really cared, who knew how to *communicate* with young people like few men I know.

Another great leader-communicator was Lewis Haws, a Sunday School teacher. My class had constant problems through the years with our Sunday School teachers. When we entered Brother Haws's class we didn't change much — at first. We were still kind of smart-aleck; we still wanted to play around and impress the girls, and they of course to impress us. But gradually we saw in our class a great teacher. And before we knew it we were gaining great lessons and getting great messages. In fact it was to Brother Haws I went when I wanted to know how you really gain a testimony. At my young age, I had not yet received a satisfactory answer; I felt I just didn't have that sure knowledge.

Finally I went to Lewis Haws and I said, "Lew, how can I really know the Church is true?"

I remember that he simply turned to the Book of Mormon and asked me to read it. He showed me Moroni's promise and said that every person who will read the Book of Mormon with a prayerful attitude may know it is true.

I remember reading the Book of Mormon, motivated by the desire to really know. I could hardly lay the book down. I would go to work, then at noon I would come home and read, then I would go back to work. And then in the evening I would come home and read it. I raced through the Book of Mormon.

With almost every page I would ask myself, "Could Joseph Smith have written this?" Of course, the answer was no; he could *not* have written it. When I finally got to Third Nephi, I remember reading about Christ's visit to America. Tears streamed down my cheeks as I gained a very special witness. I couldn't have known the truthfulness of the Book of Mormon any more surely than if I had been there with him when he visited the Nephites.

I gained my testimony because someone knew how to communicate with young people.

Because good communication often involves the sharing of deep feelings, the process is highly personal and always subject to the individual promptings we receive from a kind, loving Heavenly Father. Nevertheless there are some general guidelines that will help all of us to attune ourselves with youth. They're worth reviewing from time to time.

1. *Seek Heavenly Father's guidance* before any approach is made to a young person. Pray with all your heart and soul, and remember that you may be the one the Lord will use to activate or reactivate that particular girl or young man for whom you are praying. And when you pray, always be specific. It is of benefit to pray for the whole class, but I think the Lord expects us also to pray for individuals. Plead with the Lord and get his guidance and direction before you enter upon this sacred service to youth.

2. *Find out as much as you can* about each young person under your stewardship. Be aware of his or her hobbies, school classes, talents and skills, friends. Do some background study to be able to talk to each youth in a special, personal way.

3. *Really develop a sincere attitude of caring.* Don't be critical. Pray about that person until you truly can say that you care in the way the Savior would. One of the great overruling principles affecting most young people who have been activated, even more important than conversion or proper fellowshipping, was the fact that they knew that someone really cared.

4. *Be sincere.* Be careful not to flatter young people. Flattery is never successful; our young people can read through it in a minute. Find something that you can truly, genuinely, compliment them on and then be sincere as you pay that compliment.

5. *Stress total involvement in filling your stewardship.* Don't make it merely an assignment where you meet the youth once a week in a class, but rather develop a total interest in your young people. If they meet you only on Sunday morning

or one evening a week, they'll know you are just filling an assignment.

6. *Don't be easily offended.* Be sure that you are not offended when the youth are critical of you. They are really only trying to get your attention in most cases.

7. *Communicate spirituality.* Young people need to feel the security of those who have their roots deep and strong in the Church. Talk about very special, spiritual things; talk about those things that give them a spiritual experience, for once they have had such an experience they will never forget you.

Someone said, "If I hate you, no matter what you say, how eloquently you speak, I don't hear a word. And if I love you, no matter how clumsy your English, no matter how clumsy your ability, I hear every word."

Young people truly will respond to things of the Spirit when given at the right time. When I taught seminary for several years in Boise, my overruling objective every morning was to provide someone in my class with a spiritual experience. I never changed that objective.

8. *Help our youth to have vision,* to be able to see the overall picture. If a young man, for example at twelve, can imagine himself sitting before the bishop clean and pure and worthy, and being able to answer all the questions that the bishop may ask in a worthiness interview in the correct way and with the right answer, he will want someday to actually be in that position and do just that. To have a vision of going to the temple worthily, to serve a sacred and holy mission, to later become an important person in the kingdom — these are the pictures we must communicate to our youth. As I have talked with young people who have had their patriarchal blessing, it has become obvious that the blessing opens up visions of the future to them. Conversely, "where there is no vision, the people perish," youth stumble and lose their way and do not realize their destiny. Wise is the man or woman who can at the very vital teaching moment give vision to the life of a youth earnestly seeking to know what the future holds.

9. *Take time to really be a steward* over the total activity of the young person. Be aware of everything that is being done by every member of your class, and then participate as much as your schedule will allow.

10. *Focus on the individual.* Remember that in most cases there are one or two, or possibly three, in a class who need special attention, who need more of your time and effort than the others. Take time to focus on those individuals, and by so doing you will have a strength that will not dilute your effectiveness. As we focus on particular individuals, we begin to break down the barriers that are holding them back from full fellowship in the class or group.

11. *Work closely with others* who also have a stewardship with you over a different segment of the young person's life. Seminary teachers, institute directors, Aaronic Priesthood advisers, special project chairman may all work together to activate and motivate one soul.

12. *Expect to put tenure in your job* in the Church. It's frustrating to youth to have a teacher come in and teach for three or four mouths and then — just as real communication begins — to see that leader released and another one come in and begin all over. Many of our young people have never had a teacher or an adviser longer than six months.

This is an indictment against those of us who are priesthood leaders. We ought to call teachers and leaders and expect them to spend enough time in the calling to have profound impact upon the young people. When I was first called to be a Scoutmaster, it took many months — almost two years — before I really understood my assignment and stewardship. How then can we learn our jobs — our youth — in one or two months and then turn that sacred trust over to someone else who will do it for three months? Let's put tenure into our callings.

Many influences are at work on the lives of our young people. We would always hope that enough of these influences would be good that steering the young person in the right direction would never depend solely on one influence. But suppose that for one young person this should be so. And suppose that, as a youth leader, you are that crucial influence.

The possibility is, then, that if we should fail in our callings to serve young people the Savior may have no other plan to bring them back to eternal life. Viewed in this light, could we have a greater, more sacred responsibility than to communicate with and lead effectively the youth under our stewardship?

5
DAD – MR. EVERYTHING

All of the work done by the Aaronic Priest-hood, by the Young Women's organization of the Church, and by the bishop and his counselors, is done with one basic purpose: to assist and supplement all that the father does within his home.

"Last year, up on the Russian River in central California," recounts Jenkin Lloyd Jones in an address, "I watched a father osprey at the top of a dead tree teaching his chick how to fish. The father osprey would take off and dive like a plummet into the river in which the whiting were running, come up with a fish, and fly back to the limb, and then the chick would take off and describe a couple of clumsy cartwheels in the air and hit the water with a splash, and less often come up with a fish. And do you know what? I didn't hear the chick say to his father, 'Look, Dad, you're irrelevant.'

"Dad was the way of life; Dad was the secret of survival. And if that's good for the osprey nest, then for the sake of our nation and its oncoming generations, let's bring back Dad."

Jones decries what he calls "the worst-raised generation in the history of America." "And who raised them?" he asks. "We did! Who tried to buy their love with material things for which they were not ready? We did! Who sought to gain status by seeing to it that our kid was the first kid on the block with the new gizmo? We did."

The stark contrast of the example-setting osprey and the spineless American parent serves well to remind us of the enormous difference between *quality* dadhood and deadhead dadhood.

That contrast is highlighted by Jones as he describes Roman Society before and after the fall of the Empire. He quotes from Philip Van Ness Myers's book *Ancient Rome, Its Rise and Fall:* "The most important feature . . . of this family group was the authority of the father. It was in the atmosphere of the family that were nourished in Roman youth the virtues of obedience, deference to authority, and in the exercise of parental authority the Roman learned how to command as well as how to obey."

But not long thereafter, Mr. Jones continues, a change began taking place. He quotes from Jerome Carcopino's book *Daily Life in Ancient Rome:* "By the beginning of the second century A.D., Roman fathers, having given up the habit of controlling their children, let the children govern them and took pleasure in bleeding themselves white to gratify the expensive whims of their offspring."

"Dad," Jones concludes, "must be an *awesome* thing if he's going to preserve what he's been working for all these years. . . . Dad must be something to push against, not a feather pillow."

Indeed, Dad must be many, many things. Especially in The Church of Jesus Christ of Latter-day Saints.

For one thing, Dad is the priesthood holder. Basically, we believe that a father exists for his family, for his home. And if we believe that the greatest organization in time or in eternity is the family unit — as I certainly do — we begin to see Dad as the patriarch of an immensely important organization. Each child of God is privileged to come into a family unit, and in the Church we would hope that every child would be a *covenant* child — that is, that his or her parents would have been married in the temple, sealed by the Holy Spirit through their good works. Children born into such families are usually taught the gospel plan very conscientiously, and a love for our Heavenly Father and for Jesus Christ is just part of family living in such homes.

In these homes a child may grow, mature, and find a pattern of living that may well stand him in good faith and close to the Church for the rest of his life — if the father is doing his job.

In other homes some of our children are not so blessed. Their family possibly has fallen into inactivity in the Church, and contention and dissension may be a way of life for them. Others are born into homes where the mother and father are separated or divorced. Other young people are brought into the Church with neither parent being a member — a cause for other possible conflicts.

But whatever the situation, every father should know that the Church, by inspiration, is organized to assist him in his God-given stewardship over his family. In the organization of the Church we have what we call a "prime line." It is a line of leadership authority that extends from our Heavenly Father and his Son Jesus Christ to his prophet here on earth, who is the President of the Church. From there the line extends to the First Presidency, then to the Quorum of Twelve, and thence to the stake president. It leads from there to the priesthood quorum, then directly to the father, in the home, and then from the father to his son or daughter. A *secondary* line follows the same course as the primary line as far as the stake president, but then it extends to the bishop and to an Aaronic Priesthood quorum and to the members of the quorum, of which the son is a part. The primary line of authority, however, is through the priesthood quorum to the *father,* and hence his tremendous importance not only as a dad but as a patriarch in his own home.

Where there is no direction at home by the father, it is

the objective of the proper priesthood leaders to do all they can to help the father to become a wise steward — a true patriarch — in his home. In fact it is a priesthood leader's primary responsibility to assist the father in his stewardship over his home. The bishop, his counselors, and all leaders who work with young people will want to do everything they can to help fathers to build in the life of each youth a testimony of the gospel of Jesus Christ. This is more important than we might ever suppose, for with Dad in a position of true leadership, we find the entire family being guided in the way of truth and light. There's just no substitute for a firm, priesthood-oriented, God-fearing father in the home. Neither society, nor government, nor even the Church can ever replace the father. All we can do is substitute when absolutely needed. Our chief objective, then, should be to build the father.

As well as being the priesthood bearer, Dad is the leader. Robert Paul Smith in his book *Where Did You Go? Out. What Did You Do? Nothing* recounts a "crisis" wherein he and his two- or three-year-old son were deadlocked, each determined not to give way. He recalls:

> His mother rushed in to say that I must Gesell him a little, or at least Spock him or treat him with a little Ilg, and I went away. . . .
>
> I found him later, ready to renew hostilities, but on his face and in his manner was much weariness, much fatigue, and a kind of desperation. I had a moment of pure illumination. I stood there and saw inside his head as clearly as if there had been a pane of glass let in his forehead. What he was saying was, "Please, please, for Heaven's sake, somebody come and take this decision out of my hands, it's too big for me."
>
> I grabbed him and picked him up and carried him to wherever it was I thought he was supposed to go. He was little then, he hit me and bit me and wet me, he hollered bloody murder and did his level best to kill me. I remember now, it was to his bed he was supposed to go. I got him there and dumped him in, put the crib side up. He was in his cage and he had been put there by his keeper, and he went to sleep as happy as ever I saw him.

There were rules. Nobody was going to leave him out in the middle of nowhere trying to figure out what he was supposed to do when he was too young to know what to do.[1]

Without question children need discipline. They want it. They want to be told what to do, what not to do. They need the security of knowing the bounds, the limits of their world. And it's basically up to Dad to lay out that world in terms they can understand.

That leadership doesn't imply tyranny, or physical abuse, or one-sided communication. But it does imply a leader-follower relationship in which Dad sets the example, and son or daughter follows a recognizable trail.

I remember many years ago reading a book by Moss Hart. The following excerpt[2] tells of a great experience he had as a boy with his father at Christmastime:

Obviously Christmas was out of the question — we were barely staying alive. On Christmas Eve my father was very silent during the evening meal. Then he surprised and startled me by turning to me and saying, "Let's take a walk." He had never suggested such a thing before, and moreover it was a very cold winter's night. I was even more surprised when he said as we left the house, "Let's go down to a Hundred Forty-ninth Street and Westchester Avenue." My heart leapt within me. That was the section where all the big stores were, where at Christmastime open pushcarts full of toys stood packed end-to-end for blocks at a stretch. On other Christmas Eves I had often gone there with my aunt, and from our tour of the carts she had gathered what I wanted the most. My father had known of this, of course, and I joyously concluded that this walk could mean only one thing — he was going to buy me a Christmas present.

On the walk down I was beside myself with delight and an inner relief. It had been a bad year for me, that year of my aunt's going, and I wanted a Christmas present terribly — not

---

[1]Robert Paul Smith, *Where Did You Go? Out. What Did You Do? Nothing* (New York: W. W. Norton and Co., 1957), pp. 88-89.

[2]From *Act One*, by Moss Hart. Copyright © 1959 by Catherine Carlisle Hart and Joseph M. Hyman, Trustees. Reprinted by permission of Random House, Inc.

a present merely, but a symbol, a token of some sort. I needed some sign from my father or mother that they knew what I was going through and cared for me as much as my aunt and my grandfather did. I am sure they were giving me what mute signs they could, but I did not see them. The idea that my father had managed a Christmas present for me in spite of everything filled me with a sudden peace and lightness of heart I had not known in months.

We hurried on, our heads bent against the wind, to the cluster of lights ahead that was 149th Street and Westchester Avenue, and those lights seemed to me the brightest lights I had ever seen. Tugging at my father's coat, I started down the line of pushcarts. There were all kinds of things that I wanted, but since nothing had been said by my father about buying a present, I would merely pause before a pushcart to say, with as much control as I could muster, "Look at that chemistry set!" or, "There's a stamp album!" or, "Look at the printing press!" Each time my father would pause and ask the pushcart man the price. Then without a word we would move on to the next pushcart. Once or twice he would pick up a toy of some kind and look at it and then at me, as if to suggest this might be something I might like, but I was ten years old and a good deal beyond just a toy; my heart was set on a chemistry set or a printing press. There they were on every pushcart we stopped at, but the price was always the same and soon I looked up and saw we were nearing the end of the line. Only two or three more pushcarts remained. My father looked up, too, and I heard him jingle some coins in his pocket. In a flash I knew it all. He'd gotten together about seventy-five cents to buy me a Christmas present, and he hadn't dared say so in case there was nothing to be had for so small a sum.

As I looked up at him I saw a look of despair and disappointment in his eyes that brought me closer to him than I had ever been in my life. I wanted to throw my arms around him and say, "It doesn't matter . . . I understand . . . this is better than a chemistry set or a printing press . . . I love you." But instead we stood shivering beside each other for a moment — then turned away from the last two pushcarts and started silently back home. I don't know why the words remained choked up within me. I didn't even take his hand on the way home nor did he take mine. We were not on that basis. Nor did I ever tell him how close to him I felt that night — that for a little while the concrete wall between father and son had crumbled away and I knew that we were two lonely people struggling to reach each other.

Many such experiences come to fathers and their children during their lifetimes which temporarily "crumble the concrete walls" and cause, as in the case of Moss Hart and his father, a situation of "two lonely people struggling to reach each other."

Along with teaching the father to respond in his stewardship role as husband and father, we as youth leaders have a responsibility to teach our youth to prepare to be the kind of family leaders the Lord would have them be.

For better or for worse, too, Dad sets an example — usually *the* example — to his children. Priesthood leaders should always remember that no other person, with the possible exception of the mother, can potentially have as great an influence as can a father. We should remember, too, that in many cases a father may teach and prepare and have a dramatic effect on his son — yet the impact may not be realized until many years later. We just keep building, adding to, strengthening the principles of truth, the principles of work, the principles of success in the life of the boy or girl. And eventually, over the period of years, the harvest will begin to be realized. The cycle will be completed. Then, it is hoped, the next generation will move forward, teaching the same basic principles and doctrines of the Church concerning father and his stewardship in the home.

A verse by Colen H. Sweeten, Jr., entitled "The Soul of a Pioneer" discusses the value of a father's example through those years of hard work and labor, focusing on the masculine image that comes from a father whose priorities are lined up, whose example shines through:

> Dad's big hands could tame the land,
> He could pull out the brush by the roots:
> When luck played out on the things he planned,
> He lifted himself by his boots.
>
> The graves he dug and the hearts he cheered,
> As he struggled to till the earth,

Are all that remain, and more endeared
Than anything of worth.

Oh, the wind that tolls the lonely chimes,
Where the city folks can't hear it,
Nearly broke his heart a thousand times,
But it couldn't break his spirit.

For there was sod to turn and stock to sell,
While the West became of age;
There are rewards mere words can't tell,
When men push back the sage.

Hands made for work, they knew no play,
A heart that knew no fear;
The courage to plod on day after day —
That's the soul of a pioneer.

Where a strong father's example doesn't exist in the home, our leaders of youth share a tremendous responsibility of setting the pattern by example. I thank my Heavenly Father that I had great priesthood leaders, Sunday School teachers and Scout leaders who set a pattern that I did not find in my home, and who caused me to see something better than I had ever before seen — and to desire it urgently. Through them I have learned to pray. Through them I have set a higher pattern of living in my home than I would have attained otherwise. Through their example, I have vowed that my children would not be faced with the anxieties and frustrations which I faced in a home that was not religion oriented.

I am sure my teachers in the different organizations would never have supposed that the Lord had a great work for me to do. Yet his overruling hand across my total life has, I feel, been placed there largely through the example of those who sought to set patterns of conduct for me to follow.

Put another way, my present home does not reflect the home of my father. Rather, it reflects the fine examples of Church members I saw and desired to be like. We can indeed have a profound effect upon the lives of those whose parents are inactive or disinterested in the Church.

This verse, whose authorship is unknown to me, seems to sum up the whole concept:

TO ANY DADDY

There are little eyes upon you,
And they're watching night and day;
There are little ears that quickly
Take in every word you say;
There are little hands all eager
To do anything you do;
And a little boy who's dreaming
Of the day he'll be like you.

You're the little fellow's idol;
You're the wisest of the wise.
In his little mind, about you
No suspicions ever rise;
He believes in you devoutly,
Holds that all you say and do,
He will say and do, in your way,
When he's grown up like you.

There's a wide-eyed little fellow,
Who believes you're always right;
And his ears are always open,
And he watches day and night;
You are setting an example
Every day, in all you do,
For the little boy who's waiting
To grow up to be like you.

Additionally, Dad is the one who loves his family. Love. Unconditional love. That's what dadhood is all about. The father who has been blessed with the attitude of unconditional love will find that the fullness of life will be his and his children's. Eventually the things he holds most sacred and dear above all others begin to line up. Things such as family unity, missions, temple marriage, the value of hard work, a home as a haven of security and protection become part of his pattern and model as he reflects the gospel of Jesus Christ and makes it a reality in the lives of his family.

One of the sweet examples of unconditional love is found in section 121 of the Doctrine and Covenants where Joseph Smith cries out:

> Oh God, where art thou? And where is the pavilion that covereth thy hiding place?
>
> How long shall thy hand be stayed, and thine eye, yea thy pure eye, behold from the eternal heavens the wrongs of thy people and of thy servants, and thine ear be penetrated with their cries?
>
> Yea, O Lord, how long shall they suffer these wrongs and unlawful oppressions, before thine heart shall be softened toward them, and thy bowels be moved with compassion toward them?
>
> O Lord God Almighty, maker of heaven, earth, and seas, and of all things that in them are, and who controllest and subjectest the devil, and the dark and benighted dominion of Sheol — stretch forth thy hand; let thine eye pierce; let thy pavilion be taken up; let thy hiding place no longer be covered; let thine ear be inclined; let thine heart be softened, and thy bowels moved with compassion toward us.
>
> Let thine anger be kindled against our enemies; and, in the fury of thine heart, with thy sword avenge us of our wrongs.
>
> Remember thy suffering saints, O our God; and thy servants will rejoice in thy name forever.

Joseph needed strength beyond himself. He needed the security and understanding of a wise and loving Savior, or possibly a father. In response to this plea from Joseph, recall the words of the Savior in the seventh and eighth verses of section 121:

> My son, peace be unto thy soul; thine adversity and thine afflictions shall be but a small moment;
>
> And then, if thou endure it well, God shall exalt thee on high; thou shalt triumph over all thy foes.

In many ways our children cry out to us as did Joseph. Not verbally, always, but in ways just as communicative. We see all the signs. We know that what they really need is a loving and kind father saying, "My son, peace be unto thy soul." And if we furnish the kind of love and leadership they need, we will find new strength coming to the father, to the son, to the daughter, to the entire family. And then we will be able, through the blessings of the Church, to extend the family unit into time and eternity.

The word *unconditional* means just that. Father's love should remain constant through good times and bad, through the brilliant successes of his children and through their failures; during times of stress, and even through the heartache of transgression. He loves, always.

As Elder Marvin J. Ashton said, "We never fail until we stop trying." I might add that the dad with love in his heart will *never* run out of ways to set the example.

When love shines through, miracles indeed can happen. I can't forget this story, taken from Sterling W. Sill's book *The Miracle of Personality.*

Some time ago a story was told about a boat sinking somewhere off the Pacific Northwest coast during a violent storm. A crowd had gathered to watch the battered vessel being pounded to pieces on the rocks offshore. Some sturdy men launched a lifeboat and pulled frantically at the oars to reach the ship in time to rescue the seamen who clung to their fast-disintegrating vessel.

As the small lifeboat came struggling back to shore, someone cried out, "Did you save them?"

"All but one," came the answer through the storm. "There was one that we couldn't reach."

Then a young man stepped forth from the group and called, "Who will come with me to get the other man?"

Then his grey-haired mother cried out, "Oh, Jim, please don't go! Please don't risk your life; you are all that I have left."

Onlookers knew that this boy's father had been drowned at sea, and years ago his brother Bill had sailed away and had never been heard from since.

But the boy replied, "Mother, someone *has* to go."

A few others joined him, and together they launched their boat and pulled for the wreck, while those on shore anxiously waited.

Finally the boat was seen to pull away from the wreck and head again for the shore. The crowd watched as the small, frail craft was beaten by the waves. At every plunge of the boat it looked as if it would be crushed like an eggshell. There was silence on the shore as the watchers prayed. For an hour the desperate struggle continued, until the lifeboat was near enough to hail; then someone shouted, "Did you get the other man?"

Then in a high, clear, triumphant shout above the roar of the surf came the young man's voice saying, "Yes! And tell mother that the man we rescued is Bill!"[3]

I can't help but wonder what a strong, wonderful, *loving* father Jim would have made.

Father's love, of course, translates into many practical things. Things like just playing together. Having a quiet moment. Talking it out. Listening. In short, Dad is a pal.

The poem "Dad," whose authorship is unknown to me, comes closer than anything I know to characterizing the feelings of a little boy about what he *wished* his Dad could be.

One day when Bruce was just a lad
First starting out in school,
He came into my workshop
And climbed upon a stool.
I saw him as he entered
But I hadn't time to play,
So I merely nodded to him
And said, "Don't get in the way."

He sat a while just thinking,
As quiet as could be,
Then carefully he got down
And came and stood by me.
He said, "Old Shep, he never works
And he has lots of fun,
He runs around the meadows
And barks up at the sun.

---

[3]Sterling W. Sill, *The Miracle of Personality* (Salt Lake City: Bookcraft, Inc., 1966), pp. 112-113.

"He chases after rabbits
And always scares the cats.
He likes to chew on old shoes
And sometimes Mother's hats.
But when we're tired of running
And we sit down on a log,
I sometimes get to thinking —
I wish my Daddy was a dog.

" 'Cause then when I came home from school
He'd run and lick my hand,
And we would jump and holler
And tumble in the sand.
And then I'd be as happy,
As happy as could be,
'Cause we would play the whole day through,
Just my Dad and me.

"Now I know you work real hard
To buy us food and clothes,
And you need to get the girls
Those fancy ribbons and bows,
But sometimes when I'm lonesome
I think 'twould be lots of fun,
If my Daddy was a dog
And all his work was done."

Now, when he'd finished speaking
He looked so lonely there,
I reached my hand out to him
And ruffled up his hair.
And as I turned my head aside
To brush away a tear,
I thought how nice it was
To have my son so near.

I know the Lord didn't mean for man
To toil his whole life through,
"Come on, my son," I said, "I'm sure
I have some time for you."
You should have seen the joy
And sunlight in his eye,
As we went outside to play —
Just my son and I.

Now, as the years have flown
And youth has slipped away,
I've tried always to remember
To allow some time to play.

. . . .

When I pause to reminisce
And think of joys and strife,
I carefully turn the pages
Of this wand'rer's book of life.
I find the richest entry
Recorded in this daily log
Is the day that small boy whispered,
"I wish my Daddy was a dog."

But the one act that truly unlocks the powers of Dad to function as the patriarch of his family is his ability to pray; for that one act opens his mind and his heart to immense powers of insight and concern in guiding his children.

Indeed, through prayer the father might well expect the same kind of miracle Alma prayed for and received in the conversion of his son Alma. It is recorded in the book of Mosiah:

> Now the sons of Mosiah were numbered among the unbelievers; and also one of the sons of Alma was numbered among them, he being called Alma, after his father; nevertheless, he became a very wicked and an idolatrous man. And he was a man of many words, and did speak much flattery to the people; therefore he led many of the people to do after the manner of his iniquities.
>
> And he became a great hinderment to the prosperity of the church of God; stealing away the hearts of the people; causing much dissension among the people; giving a chance for the enemy of God to exercise his power over them.
>
> And now it came to pass that while he was going about to destroy the church of God, for he did go about secretly with the sons of Mosiah seeking to destroy the church, and to lead astray the people of the Lord, contrary to the commandments of God, or even the king —

And as I said unto you, as they were going about rebelling against God, behold, the angel of the Lord appeared unto them; and he descended as it were in a cloud; and he spake as it were with a voice of thunder, which caused the earth to shake upon which they stood;

And so great was their astonishment, that they fell to the earth, and understood not the words which he spake unto them.

Nevertheless he cried again, saying: Alma, arise and stand forth, for why persecutest thou the church of God? For the Lord hath said: This is my church, and I will establish it; and nothing shall overthrow it, save it is the transgression of my people.

And again, the angel said: Behold, the Lord hath heard the prayers of his people, and also the prayers of his servant, Alma, who is thy father; for he has prayed with much faith concerning thee that thou mightest be brought to the knowledge of the truth; therefore, for this purpose have I come to convince thee of the power and authority of God, that the prayers of his servants might be answered according to their faith.

And now behold, can ye dispute the power of God? For behold, doth not my voice shake the earth? And can ye not also behold me before you? And I am sent from God. (Mosiah 27:8-15. Italics added.)

The father Alma prayed with much faith concerning his son. So too must today's dad pray faithfully, and with much concern, over each of his children.

As Church youth leaders we should do all we can to see that Latter-day Saint homes — active or inactive — do not fail. Ours is a sacred trust and stewardship. We should fill it, and fill it well, and do all we can to effect the continuation of every family in the Church, and extend that family into eternity with a righteous father at the head, a faithful mother by his side, and children who honor and serve the Lord.

Yes, the prime line is through the *father*. The youth leader is in the highly important secondary line of defense. Together they fight the war for the souls of our young people.

6
THE ESSENTIAL
"THIRD PARTY"

Parents can't do the entire job alone. They need help from concerned, perceptive leaders who will use their influence to help steer our youth on the right course.

It was 4:30 A.M. — a full hour before my regular wake-up time. Yet there I was, fully awake, shaken out of my sleep as if by some external force. As I lay there in bed, the impression came to me that one of my seminary students was in trouble. Who it was — what the problem was — I didn't know. But I knew sleep wouldn't return, so I got up, went downstairs, put aside the outline I'd made for that day's lesson, and began to prepare a different lesson. I was driven by the impression that *something special* was needed that day. I went to 6:45 A.M. prayer meeting as usual and then to class.

As I stood before my students I told them about the 4:30 experience and said that someone there needed the lesson I was about to present.

I had barely gotten into the lesson when I looked down the second row and saw tears streaming down the cheeks of Paul Holmes. After class, the students trailed out one by one as I stood at the door. Finally, the only one left was Paul.

"I guess you could see, Brother Featherstone, that your lesson was especially for me," he said.

"Yes, Paul," I replied, "I could see. I'm sure the Lord prompted me to give you that lesson." Then he told me his story.

"At 4:30 I was awakened, too. I wasn't able to move. I felt that I was bound by evil spirits just like Joseph Smith when he was bound in the grove. I couldn't move. I couldn't cry out. I was helpless. It was many, many minutes before I cried out inwardly and asked the Lord to deliver me from this unseen enemy. And then the power left me."

He paused and then added: "During those hours before dawn I lay on my bed thinking, asking myself, Why should this happen to me? Why would the Lord permit such a thing? But you know what? You answered every question that came to my mind after that happened this morning. I want you to know I'm really grateful that Heavenly Father would answer my problems through you."

That experience with Paul was profoundly moving for both of us, I assure you. It helped to cement in my mind the power of teaching by inspiration, but also the effect that youth leaders can have in reinforcing and strengthening the influence of parents.

"Third-party" leaders I call those of us who, from a very particular vantage point, are in position to play roles of enormous significance in molding human lives.

Why does the third party frequently have such an impact on young lives? Why is he or she even necessary? Why aren't parents sufficient as guides and inspirers of young people? I believe there is at least one basic answer to these questions.

Most of our active LDS youth are that way because they have been raised in good LDS homes where they have been taught the gospel. But by the time they are teen-agers they are thinking more independently, raising questions. For the most part they admire and respect their parents. But it's also true that they *expect* their parents to teach the concepts and lessons they are teaching. Mom and Dad, they frequently feel, teach certain principles out of "duty" or out of a desire to perpetuate principles they themselves have found valid in life. Youth wonder how valid those principles are for them.

Then a third-party leader comes on the scene. If he is a good leader, imbued with the concepts and qualities we will discuss in this chapter, he will soon gain the young person's confidence, even his admiration. In response, the young person will come to realize that what makes the third-party leader admirable are the very principles Mom and Dad have been trying to teach all along. Moreover, the leader isn't teaching these principles just as a matter of parental duty, but because they add up as builders of character and, by the admired leader's personal testimony, as vital elements of revealed truth.

Obviously there is no real substitute for a good parent. But many of us can look back on our lives and recognize such third-party service — men and women who have had a powerful impact upon our lives. Theirs is a contribution that will be remembered forever by righteous parents, by their young people, and I believe by our Heavenly Father. Truly the third party has a sacred and holy trust, and the Lord has given us, as youth leaders in the Church, a stewardship in these callings.

For many years I've been convinced that some "natural" leaders seem to have been born with special, innate abilities for working with young people; the young people flock to them. But this special something is not really mandatory. I believe that our young people's basic honesty and makeup is such that they can learn to love and appreciate even those who lack special youth-oriented leadership talents. I have known many such leaders who accepted the assignment, loved and cared for the young people, and eventually had a tremendous impact on them.

Too many bishops wait for the right man to move into the ward to be, for instance, the deacons adviser. They feel that there is no one in the ward at the time who could fill the position. But if godhood is our potential, how can we suppose that a dedicated youth leader cannot become a deacons quorum adviser, or a Beehive or Laurel adviser, and relate with their charges? It may require more effort, more caring, more time by one not naturally gifted, but I have seen many such people rally the youth around them and wield an important third-party influence in their lives.

Years ago in Salt Lake City I had an experience with a young man which indelibly impressed upon me the power and influence of the third party. The bishop had called me to teach a Sunday School class, and he told me that I was the fourth teacher in six weeks — the class had driven out the other three. "But I won't let them drive *you* out," he said.

"There is a boy in your class named Jay," the Sunday School officer told me. "He's an obnoxious kid — the ringleader. If he gets out of line, you let me know; I'll jerk him out of your class so fast his head will swim."

"Don't worry," I replied, "I'll get along fine."

I've always felt that a discipline problem is usually the *teacher's* fault rather than the student's — that any teacher who really loves and cares about the youth can get through to them. At any rate, when I went to class that first Sunday morning my lesson was well prepared.

Jay was sitting at the end of one of the rows, a little radio in his pocket with a wire that plugged into his ear and another wire that went over to the radiator. He sat through the entire lesson, tapping his foot on the floor, apparently quite entertained at what was coming out of that little radio. But he did not disturb me, and I felt that I got through to the rest of the class that morning.

It was that way for several weeks: Jay didn't appear to be getting anything out of the lesson, but on the other hand he wasn't really offensive either. He didn't disturb the rest of the class, so we got along fine. Once or twice I actually thought I might be getting through to him.

Six or seven weeks after being called to teach the class, I found out that Jay had tried out for sophomore football, so I went over to East High and watched the sophomores practice. I stood there alone; no one watches high school sophomores. Jay went out for a pass, and as he came back in he saw me. He made a wide circle and came over. "What are you doing here?" he asked.

"I came to watch you play football, watch you practice," I said, "to find out if you're any good."

"Oh, you didn't come to watch me. What are you here for?"

I said, "Jay, I *did* come to watch you. I don't know one other guy on the team."

He went over to the huddle, and several times during the next forty-five minutes I saw him look over to see if I was still there. I wanted to see him do something I could talk about at Sunday School — just to talk about him. So I went back a couple of nights later and watched the team practice again. And then I had the information I needed.

When Sunday morning came, I said to the class, "I went over to watch East High's soph team practice the other night. I watched Jay. He's terrific — great hands. If he gets within touching distance of a ball, he'll catch it. He's got some great moves and he runs like a deer!"

I don't know if anyone else was listening, but I know that Jay was sitting on the edge of his chair listening to every word.

I followed up next year when Jay tried out for the track team. He hadn't tried out for track as a sophomore, so the coach said, "Sorry, Jay, we just don't need any more half-milers." He mentioned one boy who'd taken second in the state the previous year and others who were very good. Obviously he didn't need Jay.

Jay said, "I guess you don't own the track, do you?"

The coach responded, "No, but what do you mean by that?"

"Well, I guess I can come and run if I want, can't I?"

"I guess you can, but just don't get in our way," the coach said.

So Jay was down at the track night after night, sometimes during the track practices, sometimes before, sometimes after — always running, running, running. It wasn't long before they had a dual track meet, and I guess the coach was softened by this kid's intense drive to be somebody, to accomplish something. He came over and said to him, "Jay, if you'd like to run the half-mile — if you can place — I'll put you on the team."

There didn't seem to be much of a chance — they had all kinds of half-milers on both teams. But Jay got into the event. The gun sounded, and when the tape had been broken Jay had taken first place. They gave him a new sweatsuit and a nice locker, and he became a permanent member of the track team.

I don't believe I missed one of Jay's track meets during that season. I watched the newspapers and noted the times of other half-milers in other meets. Jay's time was pretty good but not as good as a lot of others across the state.

Finally came the BYU Invitational Tournament. I remember getting my wife up early that Saturday morning, telling her we were going down to BYU to watch the track meet. "It's raining," she said. "They don't hold track meets when it rains, do they?"

I replied, "Yes, they hold the BYU Invitational."

We bundled our three little boys up and got two or three blankets and drove down to BYU in our old Plymouth. I remember laying one blanket across a bench about ten rows above the East High track team. Then I put another blanket across our shoulders. We sat huddled there in the rain.

In a few minutes Jay came trotting over and stood there in front of his coach. The coach threw him an orange, and as he peeled it he happened to look up across the stands and he saw me. Something happened when my eyes met his. I can't tell you what it was. I just know that something happened.

He turned away, and in a few moments he came bouncing up the stairs and said, "What are you doing here?"

"Jay," I said, "we came to see one of the greatest fellows I know win the half-mile today."

He said, "Well, I'll do my best."

"Yes, and your best is *winning,*" I told him. "You don't know anything else. You're a great young man; you'll win."

Well, he got just a little teary-eyed, and then he went back downstairs. Pretty soon it was first call for the half-milers, then second call, then third. As they took off their sweatsuits I thought about other half-milers like the one from Pocatello, who was an excellent runner. I thought of another half-miler from Weber who'd been running right around two minutes (and in those days that was a good time). So I just offered a little prayer: "Heavenly Father, put Jay in one heat, and put the boy from Pocatello and the boy from Weber in another heat. Then Jay can win."

I watched Jay take off his sweatsuit. He was in the first heat. I looked around and there was the boy from Pocatello taking off his sweatsuit; he was in the first heat, too. I looked a little further and spotted the kid from Weber taking off his sweatsuit; *he* was in the first heat. That's the way the Lord answers my prayers sometimes.

Pretty soon they lined up. I was looking, watching. Then I saw Jay look up once more and he saw me. Something passed between us again, and then the runners were called to their marks. The gun went off, and off they raced around the turn.

The boy from Pocatello and the boy from Weber stayed side by side way out ahead of everyone else as they rounded the first turn and on around to the second turn and down the straightaway to the 220-yard line. They were twenty or thirty yards ahead of the third runner, then came two more, then another. And finally, about forty yards back, was Jay. As they came around the 220, Jay was still way back there. They came around the far end of the 330 and around the first

440, and still Jay was way back — sixth or seventh in the race.

As the two front-runners passed me I was cheering for Jay at the top of my lungs. "Get in there, Jay, get in there." Of course he couldn't hear me — there were ten thousand people all around me. As the boys from Pocatello and Weber got past the first 440, they were still far ahead. Then the other four or five came across the 440, and then Jay.

At that point Jay did something I'd never seen in a half-mile. As he crossed the 440, he burst into a full sprint. He sprinted around one runner, then around two more, then around another and another. And as they finished the 660, he had pulled up right in behind the boys from Pocatello and Weber. Then he started to slacken his pace; and as he did so, they started to pick up theirs. I thought, "Well, what a great run this kid made today! What a great heart! But he can't stay in there now."

But as the other two started to pick up the pace, he stayed with them. As they came around the 330 on the second lap around the far end, I watched him with tears in my eyes as I thought of the tremendous effort he was making. Then as they came around the far corner, the two front men burst into a full sprint, straight down the last hundred yards. And as they did so, I thought, "Well, that's it."

But as I watched them coming down the straightaway I thought my heart would stop. Jay actually began to move up between those two fellows. The runner on the right looked over his shoulder and could see Jay moving in. With about ten yards to go the Weber boy dove for the finish line and slid across it on his chest. The Pocatello fellow looked over his shoulder and could see Jay about a half a stride behind. He threw his chest out and stumbled toward the tape to try to reach it before Jay. But somehow Jay burst between the two of them and broke the tape. I stood up in the stands with tears streaming down my cheeks. I thought, "What a great kid he is — what a giant heart!"

I had the privilege of "graduating" each year with Jay's Sunday School class — fourteen-fifteen, fifteen-sixteen, sixteen-seventeen — and then my family moved out of the ward. Not long after, Jay asked me if I would speak at his missionary farewell.

After he'd been out in the mission field about a year he sent me a letter: "Dear Brother Featherstone: I'd like you to be one of the first to know. I've been called to be an assistant to the mission president here in France."

And I thought, "And someone just a few years back had told me, 'You let me know, and I'll put him out of your class so fast his head will swim.' "

In 1974, something happened in the temple I'll never forget. I met Jay coming out of one of the rooms. As I talked with him, he said, "I've been back to medical school on the East Coast, and now I've made contact with Dr. Russell Nelson. He has given me the privilege of being one of his assistants."

And I thought, "Who is this Jay? We don't know who he is yet. Russell Nelson has operated on our prophet, President Spencer W. Kimball, and has helped the Lord work a miracle on him; and here is Jay, going to work for him."

It doesn't matter whether it's Jay, or Paul Holmes, or Suzie, or Jill. It doesn't matter *who* the young person may be, or whether he's a track star, or an assistant to the mission president, or a doctor. But he or she is a person of worth, a child of God. And as third-party leaders our effect upon these youth can be tremendous.

Wherever I've lived I've somehow been attracted to helping the youth. When my company transferred me to Boise, Idaho, in 1968, I immediately went to my new bishop and volunteered for Church service. I was called as Explorer adviser, where I served until I was appointed to the high council. Not long after that our stake president L. Aldin Porter called me in.

"Vaughn," he said, "you've served on the Priesthood Missionary Committee and you've been all across the Church. You've seen some great youth programs and you know what makes them click. Now, we are having a serious problem in our seminary. Enrollment has dropped from 82 percent of our youth to 78 percent, then to 76 percent, and this year it's down to 72 percent. Not only that, but seminary is not getting *into* the young people; religion just isn't taking hold in their lives."

President Porter had taught seminary for five years and he knew the impact seminary ought to have on the young people. He now conducted private interviews with several bishops, high councilors, and stake presidency members, seeking input on the problem. I remember talking to him for an hour on this. Finally the president called me in again. "We have decided to release eight seminary teachers," he said, "and I am calling you to serve as a teacher in early-morning seminary."

At that time I was heavily involved in many things — I was busy in the Church, my daily work was very demanding, I traveled a lot. I wondered how I could possibly fit in seminary teaching as well. But I accepted the call. At the same time President Porter was calling other busy men to teach early-morning seminary as well: his second counselor; two excellent, youth-oriented bishops; some more high councilors; and other strong youth leaders.

It took courage for President Porter to release teachers employed by the seminary system and call busy leaders to take their places. But the impact on that generation of youth and their posterity would be immeasurable and endless. Truly, this stake president understood the blessing and influence of third-party leaders. Later when I was called to be the stake president I followed this same strong leadership pattern, selecting the best men in the stake to serve as seminary teachers.

On my first morning in the class, a Friday, the former teacher introduced me as the new instructor, then gave the lesson for the last time. When it was over I shook hands with all the students, then the teacher and I went out to our cars to go to work. He had parked his car in front of the meeting-house, and there it sat — with all its wheels off. Some of the students had jacked his car up, put it on blocks, taken all four wheels off, then rolled them around in back of the chapel and hidden them.

I was devastated. I had been going to work at six or seven in my company for years. Now because I had accepted this call, I wouldn't be able to get there until just a few min-utes before eight. Yet here was this teacher's car blocked up off the ground, its frustrated owner desperately trying to find the wheels. I thought that I wouldn't know what I would do if that happened to me. It was hard enough to go to work an hour or two later each day, let alone going even later than that due to practical joke delays.

Monday morning came and I taught the class through that week and the next, though not without incident. The going was far from easy, but the first weeks saw a complete turnabout. Previously these young folks had been giving the "right" answers but they weren't really sincere; now they were beginning to internalize principles of the gospel, to make them a part of their lives. They were having spiritual experi-ences; I know the Spirit bore witness. They never fooled around with my car. They were all inside listening to the lesson.

Of course the seminary teacher is in a tremendously ad-vantageous position to affect youthful lives. Think of the exposure I had as this third-party leader: for one hour a day, five days a week, I had these young people soon after they got up in the morning when they were fresh, bright and cheer-ful. And I had them in a totally spiritual setting. Through my lessons I was able to help arm them against onslaughts of evil, which ensnare so many youth both in and out of the Church.

Elder Milton R. Hunter said that when other classes seemed to crowd seminary out of the schedule, the solution for the student is easy: eliminate all the other classes, start with seminary, and then fill in the rest of your schedule. I really believe that, for seminary is the most vital class that any high school student will ever take, and a parent who lets his son or daughter miss this great and important opportunity might well handicap that youngster for eternity.

For my own part, I believe that the one quality any third-party leader must have is an absolute and sincere interest in each of the young people. The leader cannot succeed without this supreme quality. He or she simply has to be able to recognize the one in the class or group who needs special attention, and then take the necessary time to fill that need. In this connection I think of another experience I had as a seminary teacher. Because one of the wards had been divided, a class previously held in another building was assigned to my class. As this new group merged with my class it took me two or three weeks to begin to have an effect upon their lives, but by that time most of them were responding well. I noticed, however, that there was one girl I just couldn't get to. It was as though she was in an impenetrable box, and each morning as I began to speak she would pull down a little blind and close me off. I was very concerned. I thought about it, prayed about it.

Many weeks after the merger, with this girl specifically in mind, I invited just the young women to seminary one morning (the young men to come the next day for their special session). I talked that morning about those things which I thought would impress this girl I was so concerned about.

It was about halfway through the lesson when I saw tears coming to her eyes, streaming down her cheeks, and I knew that I had reached her. It has been one of my objectives in teaching or speaking never to have a group leave the meeting without having had a spiritual experience. I am sure I have failed in this many times; but more frequently, because this has been my objective, we have had a spiritual experience together. That morning I knew that this girl was having a spiritual experience.

After class, the girl waited until all the other students

had gone, then she came up to me. "Brother Featherstone," she said, "I owe you an apology. I've deliberately been shutting you out. I had heard what a fine teacher you were, but because I resented being transferred I thought: 'Well, he's not going to have that kind of effect upon *me.*' I apologize. I was wrong. Today you touched me, deeply. Thanks so much for being my teacher and showing such understanding."

Of course it was my definite responsibility to try to show such understanding, being a third-party leader who had been called to a specific position of service, a particular stewardship. But others not so called can sometimes have a profound impact on the young person's life, and such a person may in fact be the one most able to influence that life at a crucial time. It may be a grandparent, a neighbor, an officer of the law, a little league teacher, a coach, a teacher in high school; or it may be a friend of the family, as it was in the case of Gregg, the son of a friend of mine.

My friend Bart has eight children, including a set of triplet sons. As they grew up, two of these boys excelled in their school work without much parental prodding. But the third, Gregg, was not scholastically oriented. He liked to work with his hands, but it was a real labor for him to obtain satisfactory grades in subjects like math and English. His grades reflected his disinterest in academics. By the time he had reached the eighth grade, progress reports were a tense subject and a matter for constant contention between Gregg and his parents. The fact that his two brothers sailed through their courses didn't help much, either.

One day as Bart was talking to a neighbor about this situation, the other man made a rather surprising and unconventional suggestion. "Why don't you just assume I'll be responsible for Gregg and you worry about the other two?" The shocked father wondered how the neighbor could possibly be more effective with the son than he was — the boy's own father. But he accepted the offer. Over a period of time, which included horseback rides in the Uintah Mountains, occasional fishing trips, and the neighbor's real interest in Gregg, a warm friendship was built. The good neighbor never failed to remind Bart that he was enjoying his responsibility immensely. When he had gained the boy's confidence he was able to talk to him, to encourage and build him, to assure him that talented hands such as his are one of the world's great needs.

Gregg matured and developed an interest in other subjects. He graduated from high school as a Sterling scholar runner-up and would possibly have been the top Sterling scholar had it not been for his earlier grades. Meanwhile he continued to develop his natural bent for mechanics and building. As a matter of course Gregg filled a successful mission (where, incidentally, he was a great help in keeping many boats of the mission fleet in operating condition on one of the South Sea islands). He married in the temple and today has a young family and a degree in engineering. He is a partner in a growing company marketing electronic products which he has a great part in conceiving and building.

Bart and his good neighbor occasionally comment on Gregg's success. Here is a father who acknowledges his deep indebtedness to someone — a third party — who could look into that young man's life more objectively than he could, see the boy's abilities, and not be hampered and frustrated by desires and comparisons that parents in this situation would naturally have in relation to their three sons. You can be sure that Bart and his wife know the value of the unofficial third-party leader.

One of the greatest "third-party" leaders I have known is Dale Duffy. When I was a stake president in Boise I knew him as a man with great influence on the young men of that city — probably as much as any man I know. At different times he was a Scoutmaster in several Scout troops. A firm disciplinarian, he expected more physically from the young men in his troop than any adult leader I have ever known. Yet the young men responded to him, admired him, emulated him.

I recall that after my family moved to Boise there was a camporee sponsored by the Oregon-Idaho Council of the

Boy Scouts of America. The location was fifty miles away. Most troops rode in buses and cars to the camporee, but Dale had his young men hike that fifty miles with full packs in a twenty-four-hour period. They met at 3:00 or 4:00 P.M. on the day prior to the camporee, hiked until about midnight, slept four or five hours, got up and ate, then continued their hike, arriving about the time the camporee began that afternoon. In the many years Dale conducted these hikes it was rare for a boy to miss the hike. Two of my sons did that hike for several years. They were very proud of their achievement, and so was I. Every hiker's parent was similarly proud of his son's accomplishment.

It was Dale's idea to give the boys another challenging experience — floating the middle fork of the Salmon River. The troop started river running about the time my three oldest sons were in Scout and Explorer troops in the Boise Fifteenth Ward. I remember well how Dale involved the young troop leaders in planning. Few men know better the meaning of the phrase "preparation precedes power." We started preparing a year ahead of the event. Every boy who wanted to go had to earn the swimming and lifesaving merit badges and be able to swim two-thirds of a mile. Each also had to engage in the "Duffy Battle," a hand-to-hand combat with Dale Duffy in water over their heads. He made it a real challenge to see what kind of substance, under pressure, the boys were made of. During this battle, I'm sure each boy found just how hard he could fight for his life if he had to.

Dale also gave the boys hours of classroom training prior to the first float trip and followed this with the practical application of his training as the boys floated down the Boise River in preparation for the middle fork experience. In their training they learned a tremendous amount about what to do and what not to do on a river run. They listened to Dale because they respected him and knew that anything they did not understand might put their lives in jeopardy. On every trip the boys would go to a point just below Dagger Falls and jump into the chill water and float down about fifty yards. This was to take away the initial shock of falling into the water should they capsize.

We assigned a crew to each raft, with one of the boys assigned as crew leader. This boy was given total authority while on the river. Usually we would have about six rafts, with three to five boys and their gear on each raft.

I well remember one trip when Scott, my fourth son, was on the same raft with three other fellows and myself. Early on our trip we capsized — a common experience — and the raft got caught in a backwash and was being pounded by tons of water. I came to the surface and watched for my crew members to come up. I counted them. One boy came up, then another, and then a third — but no Scott. I started to feel real concern when I looked back and forth across the river and couldn't see him anywhere. Fifteen or twenty seconds is an eternity when you're waiting for your son to come to the surface. It's the most helpless feeling in the world. Finally I saw him come to the surface, and I heaved a great sigh of relief.

"What took you so long?" I yelled to him.

"My foot got caught in the rope, and I was being pounded because the boat got caught in the backwash." Then he added, "But I remembered Brother Duffy's instruction. I reached on my hip, pulled my knife out of the scabbard, and cut the rope tangled around my foot. Then I floated free."

I owe my son's life to Dale Duffy's training.

I recall Dale's leadership in yet another challenging experience for several of the boys in our ward, including two of my sons. The group decided that they would go over to Bruno Canyon, make a four-day survival trek, and come out at the other end. They would live off of the land — berries, fish, rabbits, whatever edibles they could find. My older son Dave later told me about the experience.

They arrived in the evening, climbed down the steep cliffs into Bruno Canyon, and then started the survival hike. During the hike they saw many rattlesnakes. They saw cattle that had strayed down into the canyon and gotten lost, their horns curled and twisted in different directions, with huge knobs on their legs where they had been bitten many times by rattlesnakes.

The group had some pretty fearsome experiences: they would sleep at night in a half-circle with their heads almost in the river so as to keep a snake or some other varmint from crawling in bed with them. They ate raw squawfish, ant eggs, mint, watercress, sarvisberries, and other berries they found.

On the fourth day the weary group finally climbed out at the other end of the canyon. It was in the middle of summer. The temperature was 100 degrees in Boise and higher out there on the desert. The end of the canyon was separated from the truck by ten miles of burning desert. Dale took Dave with him to get the truck. They ran and walked the ten miles in that terrible temperature. Dale told me later that on that walk he got dizzy, even began to see mirages; the two hikers were literally exhausted. They reached the truck, then drove back to pick up the rest of the fellows. On the way they hit a part of a road that had washed out; and for forty-five minutes Dale and Dave stood out in the sun and shoveled sand to fill in the road.

When Dale recounted the story to me later, he said, "If I were in trouble and I could choose any man on earth to be with me, I'd rather have your son Dave than any man I know." Imagine how this impressed me as a father! More than that, imagine how it impressed Dave as a young man to have a man he greatly admired expressing that kind of confidence.

It is this kind of third-party leadership that grateful parents will appreciate all the days of their lives. So will the young person involved, for the harvest he and his descendants reap goes on forever.

While the "unofficial" third party can have a vital influence on a young person's life, in the Church we can't leave it to chance. We must have leaders who are specifically called to serve the youth via Church youth programs, for even the youth who are most active in the Church will oftentimes need this kind of leadership and friendship. Bishops and other concerned leaders would be wise to fast and pray about the needs of their youth and about finding the adult leader to meet those needs. Having done that, what are the basic qualities that all third-party youth leaders should try to develop?

Build in yourself a strong testimony of the gospel — a firm, unwavering conviction respecting Jesus Christ as our Savior and the Head of the Church. This has to shine through to the youth. As one wise man wrote, "He who would set others on fire must first himself glow." Naturally this means living the life of a true Latter-day Saint: constant loyalty to the Church, its principles, its leaders — in word and action. Particularly as a leader of youth, you can never let down, can never risk working against the prayers that righteous parents offer for their children and for the leaders who affect their lives.

One Church member had this reemphasized in his life as he drove alone from Utah to California one night. He became sleepy at the wheel, but a deadline precluded his pulling over to rest. He decided he would stop at the next town and have a cup of coffee. One cup would never hurt him, he rationalized, and it would keep him awake and safe from accident.

At the small restaurant, habit and principle took over and he ordered a sweet roll and a glass of milk. The waitress smiled at him as she put them on the table. "You don't remember me, do you, Brother Jones?" she said. "Five years ago I was in your seminary class."

Be dedicated, persistent — qualities that are closely linked in leadership. They imply an unreserved acceptance of the call, a devoted application of time and effort, and a determination never to give up, never to slack off in guiding and attracting the young person to the higher way. The youth leader must pray and fast and think and consider — and eventually put into action plan after plan until finally he touches the one young person he wants to. He ought to strive every time he finds himself with a young person to provide that boy or girl with a spiritual experience, to teach something that will never be forgotten.

I recall a very special third-party experience that illustrates the value of "extra-mile" effort in working with youth. At the time I was general secretary of the Aaronic Priesthood Duane was inactive in the Church. I wanted specific guidance on getting him back, and I prayed for it — he was the only one I was concerned about at this hour. I went to his home, and as I walked up on the porch and knocked, out came a fine, sharp-looking fellow in a T-shirt. As he stood there in the doorway, I said, "Duane, I've come to arm-wrestle you."

He motioned me to come in. I thought I'd been had — he looked a lot stronger than me — but I went in anyway. He took everything off the coffee table, and we knelt down and arm-wrestled. After I had slowly put down his right arm, he said, "Do you do it with the other arm?" I said, "I do," so we arm-wrestled with the other arm, and I slowly edged him down with the other arm.

Then he said, "Do you Indian-leg-wrestle?" I made a great mistake and said yes. We got down on the floor, and I don't recall what happened after that except that he rolled me over about three times toward the fireplace. Then I made a second mistake and said, "Do you do it with the other leg?" He said yes, and he rolled me back from the fireplace.

After this I stood up, looked at him, and said, "Duane, we need you at church. We need your kind of person. Can you make it Sunday morning to priesthood meeting?" He looked at me for quite a while and then said, "I'll be there." And he was.

I'm not suggesting that all youth leaders should seek to become great arm-wrestlers or Indian-leg-wrestlers, but my experience in this situation demonstrates that there are many ways to reach young men and women. The dedicated youth leader will find the right way for each youngster.

Take time to fill your calling. If you were the bishop or the Relief Society president, wouldn't you be involved in that task more than one night a week and a couple of hours on Sunday? Wouldn't it be a *full-time* Church calling? Similarly, one of the requirements of your success as a third-party leader, whatever your specific assignment, is that you be involved with the young people all week long. Your calling is a sacred stewardship, and it is not the minimal, letter-of-the-law approach but rather *fulfilling the spirit* of the assignment that will draw you close to the youth you seek to influence.

Be reliable. Except in that rare emergency, a third-party leader must never disappoint youth. Frequently, after taking over a Scout troop or an Explorer post, I have set up the first camping trip or other group experience, only to find that the announcement has met with dull response. "Aren't you interested?" I have asked. "Oh, yes," the reply has come back, "but we've been through all this before. We've had our packs all packed; we've been over at the meetinghouse waiting, and the Scoutmaster hasn't shown up. Two or three hours later we've had to walk home with our packs." Then I've had to promise them from the depths of my soul that they would never have that kind of experience while I was their leader. It's a cardinal rule that a youth leader must not disappoint the youth.

Enjoy your assignment. The youth leader who doesn't turn up probably isn't enjoying his assignment. His *attitude,* of course, will probably determine whether the assignment is a pleasant one or is just drudgery. I recall the reply a bishop gave when I asked him how he was enjoying his assignment. He said, "It's so much fun it's sinful." That's the right answer, for surely we ought to enjoy our Church callings. And the youth ought to *know* that their leader enjoys them, that he loves being with them, that he is being influenced by them as much as they are by him. After all, that's one way of saying, "I care," of expressing regard for the supreme worth of the individual young man or young woman.

Recognize and appreciate your young people. A youth leader ought to look for ways to build a feeling of self-worth in the young people by giving each one recognition. If you're a youth leader and want to show you care, you can occasionally stand up in testimony meeting and share some experiences which mention young people by name, especially those who need the boost. We all recognize that not all such expressions are testimonies, but surely the Lord would understand and accept your motives, and if you keep your remarks brief you can still bear your testimony.

You should be alert for those who do well in anything worthwhile — in seminary, Aaronic Priesthood or Young Women's activities, sports programs, and so on. A candidate in a studentbody election, a young man who makes several outstanding tackles at football, a young woman who plays in the school band or is in a dramatic production — all these are prime candidates for recognition and appreciation.

Be a good "shadow leader." The Church emphasizes that, so far as possible, youth organize and conduct their own programs. That makes the youth leader a shadow leader, standing in the background to assist and guide the youth — remembering that "to throw a shadow you must stand in the light." This requires a high degree of organization, for among other things you must help the youth to be totally successful and as far as possible avoid having failure experiences.

Follow through on your responsibilities. Young people do not like carelessness in planning and organization. They like a leader who follows through, who has all of the fine traits they think a leader should have. I recall the poor example of one Explorer leader in California. He loaded his Explorer boys into his car; they went to the grocery store and bought some food and then they set off without knowing where they'd go, what they'd do. They arrived at a suitable place and set up camp. They played chess and checkers and generally fooled around. Three days later they returned home.

When asked about their experience, almost to a man the Explorers responded that it really was a poor one. They hadn't enjoyed it. They hadn't appreciated their leader. They talked about how he had lounged around and just sat doing nothing during the entire camping experience. They had expected much more — and rightly so. Young men like leaders who cause them to stretch, not to shrink.

Be ready to listen. How about willingness to listen to young people and having confidence in what they say? A wise stake president once said to me: "You know, we don't necessarily believe everything we hear from the adults; sometimes they get the story distorted. But when we hear something from the young people we can generally believe it."

I remember a son coming to me and saying, "Dad, Brother .... has a peculiar problem." He specified the problem, a very grievous one.

"Son," I replied, "don't ever say that again. I'm sure it's not so — he doesn't have those tendencies."

"Dad," he insisted, "it's true."

Still I refused to believe it — I just wouldn't accept it. A short time later another young man gave me the same information, and again I could not accept it. But about six months later the man concerned confessed to the kind of conduct the other two had already told me about. I concluded that youth know a straight story and when they talk to us they will tell it the way it really is.

There are other times to listen too, times when the young person feels the need to talk to the youth leader. If the problem is one the leader can handle and give counsel on, if it is within his stewardship, he should do all he can to assist. But cases of major transgression, or problems that may lead to a major trangression, are not within that stewardship; they are the bishop's concern. The best counsel he could give in such instances would be simply this: "Before you can be forgiven, you must get to the bishop. Don't tell me about these things; the fewer people you tell, the fewer there will be to discuss it. I would like you to go the bishop, and I'll help you make an appointment." If for some reason (and this would be a very rare situation) the young person cannot possibly go to the bishop, he or she should be advised to go to the stake president. These are the two men in the stake who function as common judges in Israel. They are the most important ones who can truly assist in this situation.

Something NOT to be. We have said a lot about what a youth leader, a third-party leader, *should* be and do, but there's one thing he definitely should *not* be and that is part of the young people's peer group. Becoming one of the boys or one of the girls depreciates a leader, robs him of his effectiveness. Our youth must know that there are lines they must not cross, and as they understand this their respect for the youth leader grows. Frequently young people will cross over the line in their associations and dealings with the leader, but in a firm yet loving way he must let them know that they have crossed over that line. This teaches the youth some of the basic principles of successful living.

Lead with love. Of all the qualities the third-party leader needs, the pinnacle and crown of them all is charity — the unconditional love which the Master taught and exemplified. Jesus taught it, for example, through his magnificent parable of the Prodigal Son: notice that the father in that story loved without reservation, without regard to the son's rebellion and lack of love. Jesus exemplified it in those words from the anguish of the cross: "Father, forgive them; for they know not what they do."

If you are a youth leader, your love for the youth won't always be reciprocated immediately or equally. Frequently your activities must be sustained merely by your desire to perform selfless service and acts of love, without any apparent guarantee of reward. This is the true charity, the pure love of Christ. Yet the rewards will come. "Whatsoever a man soweth, that shall he also reap." As we cast our bread upon the waters, so we shall "find it after many days."

I am convinced of this principle. I have worked with young people and performed labors that I thought no one would ever know about, that I thought would be totally lost after the act was performed, and I had that desire. Yet I have seen those acts make a giant circle and return again twenty and thirty years later and become a blessing a thousand times greater than the small effort it took on my part to perform the original labor.

Yes, the reward may be delayed but it will come, even in this life. It will come in the form of the missionary farewell and homecoming of the boy whose future you worried about. It will come in the temple as you watch the girl for whom you have special concern kneeling at the altar to be married for time and eternity. Such young people will soon themselves become youth leaders, reaping for you a whole new generation of rewards. The process is endless. That's why you must not fail in your leadership trust. There is just too much at stake — the eternal life of those under your stewardship.

And when this life is over, when maturity and eternal perspective have immensely heightened the perception and appreciation of us all, what will the rewards be then? In an expression which surely can relate not merely to conversions from outside the Church, the Lord speaks of the great joy the laborer will have in heaven with one or many souls he manages to bring to Christ at whatever cost in effort (Doctrine and Covenants 18:15-16). That will be the ultimate, though never-ending payoff for the dedicated third-party leader. In the words of the verse Elder Adam S. Bennion used to quote:

> Perchance in heaven one day to me
> Some blessed Saint shall come and say,
> "All hail, beloved, but for thee
> My soul to death had fallen prey."
> And O, what rapture in the thought,
> One soul to glory to have brought!

7
GROWING PAINS

We must help each of our youth to understand that they have a kind and loving Heavenly Father to whom they can turn — that indeed they also have a divine older Brother, Jesus Christ, who has a supreme interest in each of them.

Years ago our son Dave had a dog — a German shepherd who was quite old and overweight and yet was a dearly loved pet. I remember that through those years, as Heidi's time began running out, Dave was very careful to have her with him as he slept. When he slept out, Heidi was with him; in fact she was with him wherever he went.

One day when Dave was about twelve or thirteen, Heidi began to die. She would go into convulsions, and I remember Dave coming upstairs with tears in his eyes, telling me he thought Heidi was dying. Just before she died, she went out in the back yard and crawled under some peony plants. That evening when Dave went out to find her he heard her whimpering, and he crawled underneath the peony plants and stayed with her. Soon Dave's older brother Ron went to look for Dave and Heidi, and when he found them he crawled under the peonies with them. And the two brothers talked quietly together as they sat with the old dog, just before she died.

Parents who have been touched by such experiences will never forget them. This experience in particular, complete with its memory of sad, tender moments shared between brothers, served to remind me forever that deep, deep feelings course through the choice spirits of our young sons and daughters, particularly in time of pain and anguish.

The privilege of *sharing* feelings like those, of helping our youth to understand their innermost feelings, of helping them to interpret their feelings in terms of their progression through life — this privilege is among the choicest of experiences for parents and leaders of youth.

Those who have conducted studies in connection with the time spent by youth at various ages in different activities during each day, week, month and year of their lives have almost unanimously agreed that the greatest influence on children is that of *parents*. I believe very strongly that this is true. Whether it be for good or for bad, parental influence reaches down into the innermost depths of the young child's soul. If that influence is for good, it will bring a strength and a security that will remain with the child all his life. Conversely, if the influence be negative and result in feelings of hurt, or want, or lack of love, it takes a desperate effort to remove those feelings from the person's life. Anchoring the souls of our youth not only to their parents and leaders but to their Heavenly Father and to Jesus Christ will bring those souls a stability and a serenity that can be had in no other way. Ours is a great challenge, and sometimes it takes many years of effort, time and prayer to achieve the desired result.

The parental responsibility is eloquently stated in section 69 of the Doctrine and Covenants, verse 25: "And again, inasmuch as parents have children in Zion or in any of her stakes which are organized, that teach them not to understand the doctrine of repentance, faith in Christ the Son of the living God, and of baptism and the gift of the Holy

Ghost by the laying on of the hands, when eight years old, the sin be upon the heads of the parents."

While parents indeed have an awesome responsibility in raising their children, we certainly must not encourage our youth to suppose that they can lay blame on their parents for all their actions in later life. Only the Lord may do this.

At the same time, all of us who work with youth will do well to *know the background* of those youth — to come to a full understanding of the influences that shaped the life of a particular young man or young woman. Having that information, we will be in a much better position to understand our young people, to influence their lives for good.

A part of our understanding about *all* youth is the fact that they progress through certain predictable stages and have some highly defined needs in each stage. For example, the young boy becomes first his *mother's* boy and then later his *father's* boy as he learns to "walk in his father's footsteps," as a poet has said.

I wonder if this isn't what the Master meant when he suggested that "Except ye become as little children, ye shall not enter into the kingdom of heaven." (Matthew 18:3.) As parents and leaders of youth, we are literally making the footsteps that our youth will follow as they seek to inherit the blessings which are in store for them.

A boy between the ages of three and ten or eleven has an intense interest in being with his father. A father would be wise to fish and hunt, to wrestle and romp, to play games of interest with the boy — football, basketball, baseball, and any other game that strikes his son's fancy. A father would do well to portray a strong masculine image — an image of love and compassion, of firmness, of practical concern. If he does, he may well receive a most pleasant and unexpected result: as his son reaches eleven or twelve, he will begin to make every effort to please his father. The boy also begins doing things like helping his mother with the house cleaning — tasks wherein he can feel an inner reward for serving without being asked. Later, his interest enlarges to include those outside his family circle, and although his father and mother still play dominant roles, outside leaders such as priesthood advisers, teachers, coaches, and Scoutmasters begin to have an impact on the boy's life.

Then as the boy progresses through the early teen-ages — thirteen, fourteen and fifteen — he begins to grow out of adolescence and develops a need to belong to a group of his peers. This may be a quorum, a troop, a class, a gang, or whatever. The desire is there, and fortunately the Church has provided for it. But if we do not help him to fill this peer-group need by encouraging him to attend Church-oriented activities for his age group, the boy will fill it in a different way, with a different group. In that case he may well be involved in things he should shun.

Fourteen, fifteen and sixteen seem to be the most critical ages for the testing of a boy's character. This seems to be the period in which he is involved in the temptation of drugs, smoking, girls, etc. Many difficulties seem to roll upon the boy in great waves during these years.

Then as he reaches sixteen, seventeen and eighteen, he begins to emerge from the other side of this so-called problem age. As he turns sixteen we see some first evidences of maturity: he seems then to have a deeper interest in life. The wind, the thrill of walking in a rainstorm, the quiet contentment of going to a park and sitting and thinking things through, the amazement of examining for the first time in his life, really examining, a rosebud, or the leaf of a tree in the spring — all these experiences literally unfold a life that never really existed for him before. At the same time, he seems to be gathering around him (quite involuntarily) conflicts on all sides. So he requires much time to ponder and think. Significantly, this is the time when the LDS boy has tremendous quest for a testimony. He must know. Hence there are hours of deep meditation and contemplation about things of the Spirit.

These are also the years in which he is involved in debate or athletics at school or in the ward, when he begins to reach out beyond himself and have confidence. These, too, are the preparatory years that the Lord so wisely provides for a boy prior to his mission call. During the years of seventeen, eighteen, and nineteen there comes, too, a restlessness of spirit which prompts desires to cut the apron strings and leave home. Thus a mission call at nineteen seems God-given: it comes at the absolute crest of life when a young man needs the almost limitless opportunities of growth, of testimony building, of self-discipline, of learning to work, of spiritualizing his life.

But whatever the age, whatever the stage, it seems that nearly every experience unfolds a new lesson of life. And whether that lesson is truly learned depends largely on how we as parents and youth leaders help our young people to interpret, to understand, those experiences.

Some of us learn the hard way. I recall that in my early years, at about seven or eight, I found a cigar, and climbing underneath the house I leaned back and smoked it. After only a few puffs I became deathly ill. I remember staggering into the house, feeling as if I were going to die. I climbed into a tub of cold water (my mother wasn't home at the time), and after several minutes I climbed out of the tub and dropped into my bed and waited there to die. When Mother got home I was ready to confess. I was impressed that she wasn't overly concerned with the prospect of my leaving this mortal existence, but I felt sure she would miss me when I died.

Well, in a few hours and after some violent physical "upsurgings" (the most polite term I can think of), I realized that I'd had all the cigar smoking I would ever want in this life.

Times like these provide golden opportunities for us to teach lessons of great importance, preferably in the home — or, if not, by an interested third-party leader. Each youth is a person of worth, and through experiences like these — with our help — they will come to love themselves, to realize that they have a value, to sense that they are, through it all, truly God's children.

A father once told me about another smoking incident that proves how a similar experience can affect the parties involved quite differently. His two boys were standing with their friends outside a drugstore and a fellow several years older saw them standing there. As he went in he said, "How would you guys like me to get you a cigar?"

Since they all thought that was a good idea, he took their money inside and bought them all a cigar. One of the boys had a car, so they climbed in and drove around and smoked their cigars together. They promised each other they'd never tell a soul. They agreed this would have to be kept totally confidential. After all, they were all active in their priesthood quorum.

The next night the father of two of the boys called them in and questioned them. Being basically honest and straight-forward, they both admitted they'd been involved. The father gave proper direction and discipline, and they learned a lesson.

By contrast, when the other fellows who'd been part of the group heard about this they discussed the matter and vowed they'd never take the two boys along with them on a repeat performance. "Their dad's a prophet or something — he always knows when we do something wrong," was their reasoning.

Sometimes growing "pains" aren't pains at all, but rather powerfully simple affirmations of the existence of a Heavenly Father who cares. An experience in my own family is an example.

One afternoon Pat, a neighbor girl, phoned my wife, Merlene, who presided over the girls in our ward. Merlene wasn't at home, so the girl relayed her problem to our son Dave: she'd been out driving and had had a flat tire. She wasn't strong enough to change the wheel, and besides she didn't know how.

Dave immediately said, "Mother isn't here, but I'll come and help you," and then he hung up. He climbed on his bike and suddenly realized he hadn't asked her where she was. So he went back in the house, knelt down, and asked Heavenly Father to please direct him to where Pat was so that he might help her. He went back out and in full faith of a young man started riding his bike and rode directly to where Pat's car was parked. It's this kind of faith that young people have. It is so significant and so important that we must do everything we can to build it whenever we have a chance.

Often, in the intense emotional interplay of any family, we forget that feelings are shared by our *children,* too. When my wife went to the hospital to deliver our seventh child, I stayed with her through the entire process. When the baby was born I sat at the head of the delivery table, holding my wife's hand during this great miracle, and saw Merlene's great faith and strength of character as tears streamed down her cheeks. She gripped my hands as though they were in a vise, yet she would not cry out.

I went home and told the two children who were at home, Lawrence and Jill, about my experience. Lawrence listened intently (at that time he was thirteen) and then he went into the den. A little later he came out with a letter to his mother. I took it to Merlene at the hospital that night. She opened it and read something like this: "To my best loved mom: When you went to the hospital today to have the new baby, I went into the den and knelt down and asked Heavenly Father to please bless you. And when Dad came home today and told us how you just gritted your teeth with tears streaming down your cheeks and holding his hand as tightly as ever you could, and how our little baby brother was born, I knew that the Lord blessed you. And then an *unstuckable* lump caught in my throat."

Then he finished his letter to his mother, talking about merit badges and other things.

While I have never felt that our youth should be spared the pains of growing up, I have always felt that we must provide them with a clear *vision* of what life — what the gospel — is all about.

Whenever I go to a junior Sunday School I always try to give the children somewhat of a vision. I ask all of the children to close their eyes. Then I ask them if they can picture in their minds a nearby LDS temple, and I ask them to nod their heads if they can.

Then I say, "Can you see yourself standing in front of the golden door — one of those beautiful big golden doors? If you can, nod your head up and down." And they nod their heads.

"And now you can see the door opening, and there is someone inside dressed in beautiful white clothing who is reaching out and taking you by the hand and inviting you in. Who is that?"

And it never fails. The first little child who responds says, "It's Heavenly Father," or, "It's Jesus."

And then I say, "Well, I'm sure they are there because the temple is their holy house. But the person inside reaching out is your father, and he is dressed in white and your mother is with him and she is dressed in white, and your brothers and sisters are there and *they* are dressed in white.

"Now, if you live clean and pure, the time will come in your life when you will be able to go into the temple — when you will be able to be there with your brothers and sisters. But we have to live the kind of life Jesus would want us to live."

At this point, each of the children in his mind's eye can almost see this taking place. If we teach them through vision and give them this greater scope, they understand in a much larger sense. Then it is easier for them to live the Word of Wisdom, because of the love they have for their families and their parents. It is easier for them to stay clean and pure and live the other commandments. And this vision will remain with them through life, even through the times of their severest growing pains.

Sometimes we as parents unwittingly contribute to the pains of growing up. We allow unrealistic expectations to dominate relationships with our children. A while back I heard of a sweet mother whose son came home with his report card. He had five A's and a B.

The mother examined the report card and said: "Son, what happened? Why the B?"

Some time later the boy's father came home. He looked at the card and had the same inclination. But he resisted. Instead, he said, "That's a great report card, son; I'm more proud of you than I can say."

The boy took the card and walked out in the back yard. The father followed him. When they got out there the son had tears in his eyes.

"What's the matter?" asked the father.

The boy responded, "Dad, what do I have to do to make it with Mom? I was *proud* of my report card. Can't I ever make it with her?"

It's too easy sometimes to look at the dirt on the flower's petal rather than the beauty of the flower. We must resist the temptation to see only the negative.

Perspective — that's what it's all about. Not long ago one of my son's school teachers called up, concerned about his being boisterous and sometimes disrupting the class. I told her we would take care of the boy and discipline him appropriately and that the problem would cease; and that if it did not, I would appreciate another call from her.

I remember driving home, wondering how I would attack the problem. I knew my son had never been involved in drugs, had never tasted liquor or beer in his life, had never smoked, had never to my knowledge been dishonest. I knew, because I had interviewed him regularly, that he had not been involved in immoral behavior of any kind. I had never known him to tell a dirty story, to read a filthy magazine. In fact, as I appraised him on the way home, I reasoned that I must keep all of these things in their proper perspective, remembering what a great kid he was, and do what I could to help him with his school problem. I reflected that each of us went through those difficult years, and each of us didn't always measure up in one way or another. I recalled a great teacher, and then my great mother, who trusted me and loved me for my own personal sense of worth and still disciplined me when I needed it, and I remembered that I knew that my teacher, and my mother, still loved me in spite of the discipline. When I arrived home, I knew how to counsel my boy.

Someone has said that the parents of 57 percent of the teen-agers would like to leave home. Someone else has said that the problem with being parents is that, by the time you get a little experience, you are usually unemployed. The pains of growing up are probably responsible for those kinds of attitudes.

But just as night turns to day, as misfortune turns to fortune, so too can we, as parents and leaders of youth, turn the growing pains of our young people into exciting, inspiring opportunities for growth and self-understanding through the gospel of Jesus Christ.

8
THE BISHOP
AS A YOUTH LEADER

The Lord has reserved a great army of bishops to come forth in this day. They will regenerate in the lives of our youth an appreciation of the sacred importance of the priesthood.

For one bishop it was a case of boys in T-shirts and shoulder-length hair in sacrament meeting. For another it was a matter of some stolen goods at a youth outing. For a third it was a mistake in judgment about a deacons quorum president.

The experiences give us not only some insight into the day-to-day challenges of bishops and branch presidents, but provide a master key for unlocking their almost limitless youth leadership potential. Let's first consider the case of the frustrated bishop.

Don's hair was down over his ears and fairly long at the back — longer than the standard his bishop had set. He had been interviewed to be ordained a teacher, and the bishop had discussed the proper length of hair and suggested that Don get his hair cut before being ordained. Don returned home, talked it over with his mother — but didn't get a haircut. Thirty days later he still had not been ordained.

Later, when I had an opportunity to talk with the bishop, I found that the problem involved not just Don but most of that ward's Aaronic Priesthood. They came to church and filled their assignments in shirts unbuttoned at the collars, no ties. The assistant to the president of the priests quorum had long hair down to his shoulders, and the deacons passing the sacrament sometimes came in T-shirts, never with a tie or coat. The bishop told me he had four priests, all with shoulder-length hair.

In response to my question concerning the bishop's youth committee meetings he said, "Yes, we hold them monthly, but I don't have any control in that meeting; it's under the direction of the assistant to the president of the priests quorum and the Laurel president." He told me that on activity night the youth came in the shabbiest possible clothing. Shirt-tails were out, levis had bleached spots on them, the girls were in slacks or tight-fitting pants. There was just no standard in the entire youth program of the ward. The bishop was frustrated, didn't have an answer, and asked me what I would do.

Now a look at the case of the stolen goods.

During a two-ward Aaronic Priesthood and Young Women's opening social at a lakeside recreation area, a number of items were stolen from various shops that our young people had been visiting. The proprietor asked over the loudspeaker for the stolen things to be returned — no questions asked. As the announcement was made, several cars sped out of the parking lot; other young people were seen throwing objects out into the lake. Possibly two hundred dollars' worth of goods had been stolen from the shop.

Now to the case of the underrated quorum president.

"Why did he do such a stupid thing?" the high councilor asked the deacons quorum adviser. The quorum president had just asked Roger — who had been almost totally inactive and who had just started attending meetings again — to offer the closing prayer.

The adviser suggested that the high councilor speak to

the deacons quorum president. The question was repeated, this time to the quorum president directly. "Why did you call on that boy to pray? You know he's been inactive. You may offend him and then he won't come out again."

So much for stating the problems. Now let's seek some answers.

Case number one — the hair problem — demands that bishops and branch presidents have a clear understanding of *normative behavior,* or behavior that is influenced by the norms or habits of the peer group. If the behavior norm is for priesthood holders to come to sacrament meeting with excessively long hair and without coats or ties, you can be quite sure that most of the boys in that quorum will follow suit. Conversely, if the norm is to be dressed in a coat with a dress shirt and a tie, the boys will come dressed that way to their sacrament meeting to officiate in the ordinances of the Aaronic Priesthood. If the priests regularly sit behind the sacrament table wearing coats and ties and with their hair cut a respectable length, you can nearly always reckon that every priest will comply with that normative behavior.

Where such behavior is not the norm, the responsibility of the bishopric, with the help of his youth committee, quorum presidencies, and class leaders, must be to *change the norm* in the ward.

But how do you change a norm when it is so entrenched in the lives of the youth? As in the case of a California ward where priesthood boys were barred from passing the sacrament (Melchizedek Priesthood holders passed it) because of their hair length, how do you go about making a major change in priesthood grooming norms?

When a bishop calls a young leader — a deacons quorum president, teachers quorum president, an assistant to the president of the priests quorum, or any of the class presidents for the girls — it should be done with the same care, prayer and consideration after fasting that he would exercise in selecting a Relief Society president, a counselor in his bishopric, or any other important position in his ward. For in effect these young men and women are in the most critical positions in the ward and have the greatest influence — far more than some of our adult leaders.

After the bishop has prayed and fasted and has had revealed to him by impressions and direction from the Lord who should be called, a proper, appropriate call should be initiated. Let's assume the call is for the presidency of the teachers quorum.

The call should come after a thorough, searching interview with the boy's parents to see if they will support and honor this young man in his new calling. After the parents' approval, the boy is called in, and the bishop's conversation goes something like this:

"Gregg, my counselors and I have fasted and prayed and, after much soul-searching on our part, the Lord has revealed to us that he would like to have you serve as the teachers quorum president of this ward. Now, this responsibility cannot be taken lightly, and before you accept the call we want to impress upon you the sacred obligations that will be yours.

"First, you'll have twenty-four boys in the quorum. You will be their priesthood quorum president. You will be responsible for them — you'll have the stewardship to save each and every young man in your quorum, both those who are attending church and those who aren't now attending. You'll have the privilege of selecting two counselors after you have fasted and prayed as we have. And after you find out who the Lord would have serve you as your counselors, you will have these boys to assist you, along with the secretary."

Then the bishop should go into detail concerning what the job function will be, how much time it will demand, what meetings the new president will be expected to attend, how much other involvement there will be, and the need for constant awareness of the needs of the teachers. The bishop should discuss grooming standards with the president and get a commitment that the president *will* abide by the standard. Let the boy be involved in determining the standard; guide him to think it was *his* idea. And then, after a complete understanding of the job has been reached and the boy has been shown worthy and willing to receive the call, the bishop should officially call him to fill that position. After such an interview, the young man responding to the call will have a clear vision of what is expected of him.

This is highly significant in changing the norm, for in this meeting the bishop discusses the need for this young man to follow the pattern of his adult leaders: modest, conservative dress; the wearing of a coat and tie at the meetings where he is representing the Lord in his ordinances; the need to keep his hair of moderate length so as to set an example and model for the rest of the boys in the quorum. The bishop also mentions the need for the new quorum president to attire himself appropriately for youth activity nights and other activities so that the ward members — and especially his quorum members — may see the example he sets.

All of these things can be part of a highly important interview after he has been called the way the Lord would have this young man called. This makes the call significant in changing his behavior.

Another tool the bishop has is the bishop's youth committee. In our true story of the frustrated bishop, he said that the youth committee meeting was not under his direction but rather was directed by the assistant to the president of the priests quorum and the Laurel president. This is not so. These leaders simply chair the committee under the direction of the bishop; he presides and must give priesthood approval to everything that takes place in that meeting. He should make certain that he is always included on the agenda as giving direction from the priesthood leader, and then he must give that direction. He also has input onto the agenda in those matters he feels are significant.

Importantly, the bishop's youth committee is the place where the bishop and the youth can begin to solve dress and grooming problems, coming up with recommendations for appropriate dress of ward youth when they attend sacrament meeting, Sunday School, priesthood meeting, youth activity night, dances, and other functions. With this problem dumped into their laps, the youth leaders will respond quickly under the bishop's direction, giving important feedback and input that will help the bishop greatly as he attacks this problem.

Sometimes, to the bishop's surprise, the youth themselves will often come up with standards more rigid than most adult leaders would. They will find ways of implementing, evaluating, and enforcing the standards through their own age groups which will not reflect negatively on the bishopric or the adult leaders. More important, they will change the norm in the ward, for as the youth leaders change, the norm undoubtedly will change.

A third vital thing the bishop can do in changing the norms of his ward youth is to hold regular personal priesthood interviews with all his Aaronic Priesthood and Young Women's leaders. In this setting the bishop (or his counselor) discusses with the president of the quorum, the group leader, or the class president the need for certain standards within that group. Here he can get commitments, make suggestions, give assignments for a particular task for all the quorum members to work on, and then expect a report back. The deacons quorum president, teachers quorum president, or Laurel president may well take on the task of upgrading dress standards, achieving far greater results than if the bishop or the adult leaders tried to do it without the support of the youth.

Another vital thing a bishop can do is to make certain that he and his counselors attend every prayer meeting and every opening exercise, as well as classes and activities on youth activity night. He ought to be involved in athletics, in sports, and in camp and service projects where he can come to know the youth better. His presence in these meetings, where he will be appropriately dressed and attired, will have a great impact on the youth and will lend dignity to every gathering he attends.

Now to case number two, in which some two hundred dollars' worth of items were stolen during an opening social.

Before I make some suggestions on how such an incident might have been prevented, let me tell you how it turned out. You will recall that two wards were involved. Members of both wards were extremely concerned and very anxious to right the wrongs.

The first ward decided to make full restitution to the shopkeeper. But they went further, conducting an in-depth survey to find out just who was involved. It turned out that four young men and three young women, several of whom did not normally attend youth activity nights or Sunday meetings, were the offenders. After passing on to the bishop the names of those responsible, the youth leaders contacted the owner of the shop and told him they would like to come out to the recreation area and spend three hours cleaning, repairing, painting and mowing — generally sprucing up the place — in addition to returning as many of the stolen items as they could and paying for the rest. Needless to say, this was acceptable; the proprietor was very impressed.

The second ward, in which two young men were involved, followed a slightly different pattern in participating in the restitution. In this case the young leaders offered the names of the guilty parties to their bishop, but with one reservation: "We want to do all in our power to persuade them to come in on their own. We think it would be better this way for them," they told their bishop.

Truly, when we let the youth exercise their appropriate and proper stewardship we really begin to see things happen. Behavior changes. Youth norms change. The ward or branch changes for the better.

Now back to preventive measures: What might the bishops have done to entirely avoid such an incident in the first place? Here are some suggestions.

First, by revelation, the first and foremost responsibility of the bishop of the ward is the Aaronic Priesthood — the youth. He should be involved both with the Aaronic Priesthood young men and the young women ages twelve to eighteen. But of course the Aaronic Priesthood isn't the only responsibility a bishop has. He is responsible for the welfare of all the members of his ward, he is the presiding high priest, he is responsible for the collection of tithes and for other finances, and he is the common judge in handling the transgressor and other matters demanding a judgment.

How then does the bishop, already heavily loaded, find time to become personally involved in the Aaronic Priesthood and Young Women's program? The answer is, with the help of his priesthood executive committee, on which he serves as chairman and which is comprised of the priesthood leaders, the ward executive secretary, the bishopric, and the director of the Aaronic Priesthood. If these men will rally round the bishop, truly support him with all their might, they can take much work off his hands and leave his time freer for his major responsibility — direct involvement with the youth.

We realize of course that it isn't easy to communicate with young people. It's easier for a bishop, on the activity night of the Aaronic Priesthood, simply to slip into his office and carry on an interview, conduct other business, open his mail, assist in the finances and the preparation of agendas, or go out visiting the widows and others within his ward. These things are all important, but they are of a lesser priority than the Aaronic Priesthood and young women. It isn't easy for a bishop or any other youth leader to walk up to a young person and have him or her simply hold out a hand like a wet fish and look in the opposite direction. It isn't easy to have him or her whisper about you to a buddy in a critical way. It isn't easy to go in and really be involved with the youth. But being involved is the bishop's responsibility.

And why? So he will know what's happening with the youth in his ward. So that he will have a strong personal influence in the things his kids are doing. So that his Aaronic Priesthood bearers and young women will not be pilfering goods from the shop during a youth activity night at the lake.

Another invaluable means of getting close to the youth is through youth leaders — individually. This is done in a monthly priesthood interview with every quorum president, assistant, or class president in the Aaronic Priesthood and Young Women's organization within the ward. President Marion G. Romney has said, "The greatest tool we have in the Church to get the Lord's work done is the personal priesthood interview." I really believe that.

Can you imagine what a profound effect it could have on a president of a deacons quorum to be invited to a properly held priesthood interview? As he comes in, the bishop invites him to kneel down, and they have an opening prayer — one the deacons quorum president may be asked to give. When he finishes his prayer, the president is complimented by the bishop. Then they sit and discuss for a few minutes some complimentary things — in church, school, or athletics, possibly — about the president. Then the bishop perhaps says to the boy, "Now, President, would you list the boys in your quorum on your planning and report form?" The deacons quorum president would comply.

After they are listed the bishop might ask, "Now, how many of these are active in the Church? Tell me about each one of them." And the deacons quorum president would report on his stewardship concerning each of the boys, some of whom might be inactive. The bishop might then say, "Now, President, what can you do to activate these boys?" And the president would probably respond, "Well, what do you think I should do?"

"Well," the bishop might reply, "I would like to recommend something, but it's really your stewardship and your responsibility. The Lord will give you help and inspiration in dealing with the members of your quorum. Do you have any ideas?"

So they begin to talk. Pretty soon the deacons quorum president has an idea of an activity or an athletic opportunity for one of the boys. The bishop responds warmly, affirmatively: "Now you're getting the message; yes, the Lord is impressing you with the idea." After they have discussed each member of the quorum, the bishop may suggest that the president might want to discuss some of these things with his presidency and at the youth committee meeting during the month. They might talk about a few other things and the bishop might stress some counsel to the quorum president concerning personal worthiness, cleanliness, or ways to avoid getting involved in dirty stories, drugs, or Word of Wisdom problems.

At the close, the bishop might say, "President, would it be all right if we knelt here in prayer? I'd like to say that prayer."

Then this young president hears his fine bishop plead with the Lord for guidance and direction of this quorum and its fine young leader. He hears his bishop asking the Lord to expand him beyond his years and give him impressions and inspirations as to how to activate the boys within his quorum. The bishop concludes his prayer, and the deacons quorum president gets up off his knees about a foot taller.

Now multiply that kind of an experience by the other leaders of the Beehive, Mia Maid and Laurel classes, as well as by the teachers quorum president and priests assistant, and you begin to appreciate the lift that interviews like this can give to our youth leaders, and how they, in turn, can influence their peers to hold their heads high in gospel living.

Another task the bishop must perform faithfully is the annual worthiness interview with every young man and woman in the ward. This interview should be sacred in its tone. It would be well for the bishop to invite the young man or young woman to come dressed up in his or her Sunday best, and then in the bishop's office out in front of the desk, or side by side on the sofa, to take the necessary time to counsel, to discuss, and to interview each youth for worthiness. This interview can be one of the most inspiring and motivational experiences in the life of a young person. How can that person forget the most important ecclesiastical leader in the ward — the presiding high priest — taking time from his busy schedule to focus completely on him or her? This is a key factor in every bishop's success. How he approaches this may well determine his success as a true leader of youth.

Our third case, the high councilor who chastised the deacons quorum president for calling on a nearly inactive member to offer the closing prayer, turned out better than one might imagine.

"I almost got sick when you asked Roger to pray," said the high councilor. "You know this is only his second time out in months."

The deacons quorum president was patient in his response. He quietly replied: "I spent two nights with Roger this week teaching him how to offer the closing prayer so that I could call on him. He was ready."

This is another excellent example of what can happen when we let the youth lead out. More often than not, when given the opportunity they simply lead in a way that accomplishes a great deal more good than we adult leaders could, creating ever-stronger norms of youth conduct.

As General Authorities we constantly see norms that are created in different stakes. We see some stakes where the priesthood is dignified and all the young men are appropriately attired and dressed, clean-shaven with reasonable length of hair, and dressed after the pattern and the model of the prophet and the Quorum of the Twelve — the young women being dressed modestly, neatly, attractively.

We must have confidence in these young people, giving them direction, leadership, and a model of behavior. But at the same time we must put the responsibility and the stewardship of youth where the Lord has placed it: upon the shoulders of the priesthood quorum president, the assistant to the president of the priests quorum, or the Young Women's class presidents. The wise bishop will encourage and inspire these young leaders and bless them with his presence and with the keys of his calling in the Aaronic Priesthood.

The greatest vision the Aaronic Priesthood presidency of the wards — that is, the bishoprics — can possibly have concerning their stewardship is to eventually be such wise and faithful stewards that every Aaronic Priesthood holder will go into the elders quorums as active elders in the Melchizedek Priesthood and every young woman will remain vitally active after she leaves the Young Women's program of the Church.

As we place our priorities correctly and labor directly with the Aaronic Priesthood and the young women first and foremost, things really begin to happen. After all, we have the stake to assist us with its many activities. We have our service and activities committees, with athletic directors and specialists called as needed to assist us. We have this battalion of loyal and faithful youth workers who need to hear that "certain sound" from the trumpet's call.

Our bishops can issue that certain sound. And the strongest admonition we could give would be to urge you bishops to be directly, urgently involved in the Aaronic Priesthood. As president of the priests quorum you personally may want to hold many class instruction experiences where you are the teacher — possibly once a month or maybe even more often. The more you are involved, the greater your impact will be; after all, no one else has the mantle of responsibility for this particular assignment except you.

In your calling as bishop, along with that of your counselors, you may note that the role is shifting somewhat back to its original moorings, tying the bishop in to his chief and foremost responsibility, that of the Aaronic Priesthood. Surely in the preearth life, you as a bishop were foreordained to this high and holy calling. You were one of those special bishops reserved to come forth in this day when this great purification of the Aaronic Priesthood continues to take place, where preparing young men for the Melchizedek Priesthood becomes a significant part of your Aaronic Priesthood activity.

As one of those great hosts of bishops prepared before the foundation of this world, you have an awesome responsibility. Do all you can. Delegate all matters which can be delegated to your counselors, your executive committee, and others with whom you are involved. But remember that you must not delegate your stewardship over the Aaronic Priesthood. If you do, you will not be successful as president of the Aaronic Priesthood — the most important part of your calling.

9

COACHING
FOR ETERNITY

A coach who has principles, who has enthusi-
asm, who loves young people, can change lives
as few others can.

It was my first night with the boys as their Explorer
leader, and I'd called a special meeting. As we sat there looking each other over, sizing each other up, I saw they were
generally husky fellows — strong, athletic. With basketball
season approaching I asked them how they had done the
year before as a ward team.

"We've never done anything in basketball; we're at the
bottom of the stake," responded one of the boys.

I asked them a few other questions, and we stopped
long enough for me to arm-wrestle each boy in the post. Then
we talked — all in a very low profile — about our plans
for the post, about things we might do.

Toward the end of the evening, after they had gotten
to know me a little, I began to plant an idea into the hearts
of these young men. I asked them if they had ever been to
the area basketball tournament. They said no.

I said, "This year we are going to Area."

Of course, at first the idea was so ridiculous that most of them just laughed. But over the next few weeks as we began to go about Explorer activities and as we began to develop our basketball team I kept replanting the idea. (I was not the coach; I merely assisted, as an Explorer adviser should.)

By the end of that season we had won in the stake and in the district: and in the zone we lost the final game, preventing us from going to the area tournament. Now of course the team were disappointed. They had achieved far beyond what they had originally thought they could, but once they had caught the vision they were confident they could go all the way. And I kept building and nurturing this idea. The following year, with a clear vision of their potential, they *did* go to the area basketball tournament.

I'll never forget that final game. These young men dropped far behind — almost to where it was ridiculous even to suppose that they were matched with the other team. And then in the last quarter all of their previous teaching and training came forth. I saw these young men make forty-one points in the last eight-minute quarter. They came within just a few points of winning the game.

The idea of giving young men and women a vision is as important a part as any phase of coaching. In Proverbs we read, "Where there is no vision, the people perish." Our prophets have held a vision of what ought to be done to build the kind of life to which all Latter-day Saints should aspire. The men who have moved this great, marvelous world have been men of vision.

We must also remember that vision is often based on *discontent*. The weakling sits idle, groaning and whining and blaming others, but great men — and great coaches — set about to change things, to change the course of lives.

As far as our Church is concerned, the vision we are talking about has a very sharp focus: building testimonies. It is essential that during our service as coaches we build testimonies in the lives of the youth.

Needless to say, example by members on the team as well as by the coach will prove to be invaluable in this area. I recall Paul Hansen, a great youth leader for many, many years. During his time as athletics director and co-ordinator for the Edgehill Ward gym in Salt Lake City, thousands of boys have gone through the gym, and they all know Paul Hansen. His single objective as he met every boy was to build them, to build testimonies in them. He would often get the boys together and then ask them, "Why does the Church build gymnasiums and cultural halls?"

As the boys would ponder, he would answer, "To build testimonies, to save souls, to develop citizenship. The salvation of every young man who plays on this floor is the reason we build gyms and cultural halls and have athletic programs."

I recall that when I was an Explorer many years ago, Paul was quite a young man working at the Edgehill Ward. My team was invited to play in a regional basketball tournament, the games to be played at Edgehill Ward gym. I was second-string center.

The first-string center didn't show up and I played the position, although I was only about five feet ten at the time. I lacked confidence; I hardly dared shoot. But through my activity in high school football I had become extremely fierce competitively and would hustle and play as best I knew. I remember that after the first game (which we had won) we went back to play the second game a few nights later in the quarter finals. I'll never forget walking through the door and glancing at an announcement sheet of the games, which contained also a rundown of the previous evenings' highlights. Suddenly I saw my name. I remember the words as though I had read them yesterday: "Did you notice the improved floor play of Vaughn Featherstone?" Those few words caught hold of me and made me someone for a few moments.

Later on, when we moved into the Hillside Stake, I became far more closely acquainted with Paul Hansen. He has learned how to motivate and to save souls through athletics as few people in the Church have done.

I certainly would not pretend to be a professional coach, or to have that kind of expertise. But I have discovered a few pointers over the years, and I believe that in a small way I understand some of the ways in which coaches of both boys and girls can focus their energies on building better youth. They involve principles and skills. Here they are:

Encourage self-discipline. Many young men with great talent never really make it in high school athletics. Conversely, many others with seemingly little talent end up playing first-string varsity, making the all-state team. What is the difference? I believe that generally those who play do so because they have a white-heat desire to play. When you want something with all the intensity of your soul, this dwarfs other things in importance.

The desire to play obscures such things as dating, school politics, just being one of the boys, and fooling around. Self-discipline takes over, not because of a "have-to" attitude but because of a "want-to" attitude.

In the days when I played football I didn't have much confidence, but I wanted to play almost more than anything else. The coach told us to eat a lot of beans and drink lots of milk. I didn't like milk but I drank it. I really wasn't all that hot on beans, but I persuaded Mom to cook a pot as often as I could. The coach said we were to be in bed by 9:30, and I was in bed by 9:30. None of this was hard to do because the desire to play overshadowed all these little things. One thing the coach asked me to do that I couldn't do was work out on Sunday. He had asked each player to do calisthenics on an individual basis on Sunday. In this thing, I followed the teachings of the Church.

At regular football practice I would do all the calisthenics and put into them everything I could. I felt that I needed to do more than the other fellow because he had more talent than I did. I only remember missing one football practice in three years, with the exception of when I broke my leg. The one practice I missed was for my grandmother's funeral.

For four weeks after I broke my leg I would go out and watch the team play. After four weeks I persuaded the doctor to take the cast off, and six weeks after my leg was broken I played in another game.

I mention such things because I learned some great lessons from athletics, lessons which have helped me through life. The young man who wants to play in high school athletics has got to discipline himself. The coach can lay down rules and regulations, but without self-discipline these only result in bodily action. With self-discipline a person puts his heart into the program instead of just getting by.

Self-discipline imposes the need for self-motivation. I recall working in a grocery store during the summer, while some of the other players took construction work. I felt a need to make my eight hours work a day as strenuous as theirs. I would force myself to run from one task to another. I would lift hundred-pound sacks of potatoes and put them on a cart. Then I would push the cart with five hundred-pound sacks to the display and dump them, trying to hold the sack shoulder high with it hardly touching my body. When football season came I was in great shape physically.

Teach them to learn from others in this way. I had an older brother whom I worshipped. He played football for South High School in Salt Lake City and was my hero. I would polish his football cleats before each game. I would wash his white shoe laces and press them. No one had better looking football cleats or shoe laces than my older brother.

The summer before I went to high school he took me out to the back yard. I put on shoulder pads and a helmet and he would try to run over me. I shouldn't say try — he did. We would hit each other head-on, I would tackle and he would carry the ball. Then after a while we would reverse the procedure and I would carry the ball and he would tackle. After doing this a few nights with him (he weighed about 185 pounds and I weighed 155 pounds), do you think I had any fear of those my own age? He suggested wind sprints to build up my speed and timing. He encouraged me to run long distances to build up my wind. We would do push-ups, sit-ups, chin-ups, etc. The interesting thing is that it was hard work but I wanted to do it.

Through the years I have listened to those who have counseled my boys in an attempt to help them improve. If a boy thinks he has all the talent in the world, he's not too receptive to listening to a "has-been." It is also true that people will stop trying to help him. But the young man who listens after a game when someone suggests how he might improve doesn't only learn more, he has more people pulling and praying for him to succeed. If I were a coach, I would say to the players: "Don't be touchy when someone constructively criticizes you after a game. Listen carefully, thank him, ask if he saw anything else in which you could improve. Remember what he tells you, put it into practice, and you'll find your game will improve and so will your popularity. This is a good principle to apply to life. Be grateful for those who correct and constructively criticize you. They really have your interest at heart."

Here are a few ideas I have heard passed on to some good basketball players:

— Shoot one hundred free throws every night.

— Stand near the wall and jump up two hundred times tipping a basketball against the wall.

— Hold a basketball in your hand all the time you watch TV or sit and talk (you really get a feeling for it).

— Practice dribbling every day for fifteen minutes on the basement floor.

— Every night, just before going to sleep, think of taking fifty free throws.

I remember one of the great bits of advice I received while playing football: Whether running or playing defense, at the last instant you can choose whether to put every particle of effort into the tackle or the running drive or to relax and ease off. Those who ease off get hurt. Those who give it everything, play. Someone told me of the swim coach at Yale who a few years back had a swim team which was breaking world records at every meet. The coach was questioned about this. How were they doing it? He said, "I have taught my swimmers how to break the pain barrier." I was impressed by that statement.

Teach them sportsmanship. A boy who learns the art of the game — who becomes a technician, a mechanic in his particular sport — but does not learn sportsmanship, becomes a cancer to the game. The coach, in his initial planning and preparation for the season, should let the boys understand what he expects as regards sportsmanship. And should a boy get out of line, he should be pulled out of the game. In all my observation of Paul Hansen as a coach working with boys, I have never known him to develop a team that wasn't composed of superb sports. If a boy knows he'll be pulled out of the game if he doesn't comply with the rules or even if he reflects poor sportsmanship, the boy will comply. In most young men the desire to play is so intense that they'll do almost anything to be able to participate. The coach can use this great principle of sportsmanship to motivate and develop boys.

Boys who are taught sportsmanship will perform better than boys who don't. Those who rant and rave, who throw the ball down, who give nasty looks to the referee or the coach or the other players, or who criticize each other — those fellows do not enjoy the game. They come away frustrated if they lose and in the process they are confirmed in one of the most damnable untruths in the world: that it is always someone else who is to blame. So the coach who does not teach the proper understanding and philosophy of good sportsmanship does each person under him or her a great disservice. In the Church we should teach the value of sportsmanship and it ought to be part of our practice; we should never let our young men and women play without teaching them this great lesson. And I would emphasize that it can be done in a way that is fair to all and the treatment is universal and impartial.

Most of my sons have been involved in athletics either in high school, in the ward, or in recreation leagues. Long before the game has started, very early in their youth, I have always told each one that if he ever gets out of line I personally will pull him out of the game if the coach does not. Each one of my sons knows that I will do that if there is a default in any way in his sportsmanship.

I might add here that good sportsmanship is not only of moral value but of utilitarian value as well. There comes with those who are good sports a serenity, a self-control, a discipline which will carry them through the greatest moments of anxiety during the games. Those who do not have this self-control begin to lose their composure and to go to pieces. They become super-critical and their performance during the game simply declines to the point where they shouldn't even be involved.

Everything depends on the coach. I have never known of a team whose coach taught and believed and practiced good sportsmanship and the team didn't do the same.

Teach them principles of living. I know of a "great" coach — one of the best-known college coaches of all time. He has taken national championships, and if his name were mentioned here it would ring familiar to most readers. I also know two of the young basketball players — both of them exceptionally prominent — who played on his teams and who have gone into professional basketball. But sadly, both of these young men have made statements on television that were opposed to nearly every moral value in which we believe. It seems incomprehensible to me that a man can coach a player for four years and not teach him the great principles of life.

A good coach usually comes in contact with the young men up to three hours or more each day. In three hours, along with teaching the sport, he should be teaching principles of citizenship, manhood, hard work, dedication, dependability, loyalty, integrity, character, patriotism, morality. All of these principles for living can be taught to a young man or young woman. And they *should* be taught if a coach is worth his salt.

Here are some specific principles I believe coaches should pass on to the young LDS athlete:

— The athlete with a spiritual commitment has a well of reserve deep down inside of him which he can call on when in need. Make prayer a vital part of your training.

— Live the Word of Wisdom. Make a total commitment to it. It offers special blessings of health and other hidden treasures of knowledge. You lose in many ways if you break the Word of Wisdom.

— Keep your heart and mind pure. Sir Galahad said, "My strength is as the strength of ten, because my heart is pure." Those who are pure in heart, who do not feed their minds out of mental garbage cans, who do not listen to dirty stories, who keep their thoughts clean — they will find strength that others do not have.

— Never profane the name of God or his Holy Son. Oftentimes in athletics there are those who do this. The young man who controls his tongue will never profane the God whom he may need to call upon under real stress.

— Always treat young women with dignity and respect. The immoral, uncouth athlete has dissipated his strength in the lustings of the flesh. No one who is immoral is great. God will not be mocked, and those who violate the moral code in any degree will reap the whirlwind.

— Never find fault with your opponents or team members. If you do, they will become your enemies and will set out to destroy you. Be complimentary to them; build them up. Every time you lift someone up the ladder of success, you get a little closer to the top yourself.

— Never want anything so intensely that the person who has the power to give it to you can control you. This is true of athletics as it is in life. Integrity in athletics is vital.

— Be constant in all seasons. The athlete who is not dependable is useless.

— Select your friends with care, for you will be judged by your associations. Don't travel with the group that is crude rough, and dissipated.

Know the game. A coach must know the game. He doesn't have to be an expert, but he ought to do his homework, to study his manuals and handbooks, to know enough that at least he isn't the reason for his team's losing.

There are those who know the game, and when they see a young coach who makes some outstanding decisions during critical periods of a game, they'll let you know it and they'll appreciate your expertise in coaching. They don't expect you to be professional; but as we have said, neither do they expect you to have the boys lose because of your lack of knowledge of the game. We must know something about the game if we are to coach.

Be dependable. A coach should never miss a game or a practice except in an emergency. In my leadership of boys, I have made it a practice that when I had promised I would be somewhere with them I would not fail to meet my commitment. As a coach, when you set up a practice time you ought to be there — on time. You ought to have the gym open, making sure that everything is ready to go. The boys shouldn't have to come in and stand around waiting for someone to show up with a basketball. Dependability is a character trait in a coach for which there is absolutely no substitute.

To win or to play? It is wise for coaches to call the entire team together before the season begins and let them decide whether they want every boy to play equally, or whether they want to win. They will nearly always vote to play to win, and this is as it should be. Young men and women need to learn competition; they need to learn that Satan is going to try to knock us down time and time again, that there is a great competition going on for the souls of our youth. We need to learn to be competitive and how to get back up again once we are knocked down. Parents and others may complain when some of the players with less talent do not get to play; but the team members will defend the coach, saying, "Well, we wanted to win and the coach had the five best in."

At practice, though, and in games when the team is ahead, the coach should be wise and let everyone play and practice all he wants. If there are fifteen players and only a single team, one option is to have three teams of five each, keeping the teams rotating so that no player sits out the whole game.

But regardless of the enthusiasm for winning, regardless of the vote of the players to go for the win, let us remember as coaches that our *first* responsibility is to develop young men and women. Winning is important. And learning to win is important. But in the final analysis, these are secondary to the larger task of developing strong young Latter-day Saints.

Be an example. We have already talked somewhat about the example of a coach, but we can scarcely say enough on this. The coach must be many things: a good citizen, family oriented, with high morals and high ideals, firm in discipline and under control at all times. And in the rare case where he makes a leadership mistake, an apology should immediately follow. A good coach always attacks the *action* and never the player, and always in such a way that the individual involved responds to the criticism rather than rejecting it. Young men and young women will watch for their coach in sacrament meeting, in Sunday School, in other Church activities. They will pattern their lives after him or her as an exemplar. As I suggest elsewhere in this book, he or she may, after all, *be the only plan the Lord has* to save one of the youth.

Arrange those "special moments." It is our responsibility as coaches who work with young people to provide *spiritual experiences.* Before every practice, every game, the coach should take a few minutes to relate some story that drives home some principle in a way that indelibly prints it upon the mind of each team member. These moments should be preplanned, carefully prepared. They must not be left to chance. A wise coach also includes prayer during both practices and games. Many of the young people on the team will be those who do not pray regularly at home. Possibly 50 percent of them will be in such a condition. A wise coach will call upon those who have had experience in praying and will then quietly approach those of whom he is not sure, before inviting them to pray before the group.

Relate Church leaders to athletics. It would be well to let our youth know that many of the great leaders of the Church have been involved in athletics. President Ezra Taft Benson and President Marion G. Romney played on opposing high school teams. Many of our General Authorities even today are enthusiastically engaged in tennis, handball, paddleball, track, and other sports. They have learned to keep themselves in good physical condition.

Our youth, many of whom may never play first string, must still understand that their participation in sports is an excellent opportunity for them to stay in good physical condition, to improve their coordination, and to develop habits of health for life. One day they will be grateful for this.

Use athletics as a missionary tool. Church athletics can be used very effectively to activate members and to stimulate nonmembers to participate. There are those within the boundaries of your branch, ward or stake who can get very excited about athletics, who would love to participate, who will do all they can to be involved. Your invitation for them to participate might well be the "rope" with which they are pulled into the Church or, if inactive, back into activity. Many of our fine nonmember friends feel very *much* at ease on a basketball court and very *ill* at ease sitting in a meeting with us — until they have some friends who attend meetings. One of the prime targets of the coach, then, should be to activate inactive members and to baptize (or at least fellowship) nonmembers.

Never underestimate your young people. Many a scrawny, spindly-legged young man or woman has had such an intense desire to be someone that, unbeknown to the coach, he or she has gone home and practiced hour after hour on a hoop or dribbled the ball to try to gain some expertise. Someone has said, "It isn't the dog in the fight that counts, but the fight in the dog." Most young men and young women are, after all, motivated to participate in athletics with the hope of *being* somebody, being important to their peer group, being important to their parents and proving to themselves that there is a sense of worth in each one of them.

I had a very good friend, Terry Nofsinger, who had not attempted to play football during his first two years in high school. In the third year he went out for high school football, but the coach wouldn't even give him a chance to try. I don't believe he played more than three minutes of one game during the entire season. He played either third- or fourth-string quarterback in his high school senior year.

The next year he went to the University of Utah, where of course he was totally unknown. But the coach there had a greater sense of fair play, and even though many of his players were there on scholarships or had received acclaim during their high school years, he let Terry play. Before the season was half over, Terry was playing first string on the freshman team. They had a great year that year.

Terry went on to become all-conference quarterback during his senior year in varsity football, and then played professional football for Pittsburgh, St. Louis, and Atlanta. Some coach back in high school had simply underestimated him.

Handle the "pros" properly. There is another group of young men and women of whom we must be mindful — the ones who are so good that they play for the high school teams. Coaches ought to use these young people in our ward athletics, but they shouldn't dominate our Church sports program to the detriment of those who get to play only at church. They may become assistant coaches; they may be able to sit on the bench and give the coach some ideas. But the coach should try to take time to watch the games in which they play, and then in Church meetings praise their performance. Also, a letter of praise may be written in some cases where a school athlete has performed in an outstanding way — one from his bishop or stake president that he can put in a book of remembrance.

Let's remember that our athletes may well be the leaders in the ward. And they will lead either for good or for bad. The talent is there, and if we do not use it in a positive way Satan may use it in a negative way.

Give special help where it's needed. Those who are in school athletics sometimes need special attention from you as coach. Talk to them individually and find out what their needs and problems are. Occasionally a good performer who makes consistently eighteen or twenty points in a game will drop down to a game or two where he makes four or five points. Someone who will take time to help may well prove to be a blessing to the boy.

I remember one young man who had been an extremely high scorer on the team, and then he went through two or three games in which he scored less than ten points. An adult friend invited the boy down to go to the ward gym late one evening. They practiced for probably three hours, the leader just continually passing the ball to him and having him shoot from all over the floor. Then he had the young man shoot over a hundred free throws. Practice, practice, practice. As he continued to shoot constantly for three hours, his attitude changed and he picked up the confidence he needed. In the next game he went right back again and pulled up to his normal scoring position in the high teens and low twenties.

When my son was playing ball, our great friend Bishop Marvin Peterson of Boise suggested, "Dave, one of the most important things you can do right now is to take a hundred free throws every single night." Dave did this; he didn't resent that someone had told him how to improve his game. He simply became like a sponge during that senior year, and every time someone told him something they knew would help him, he tried it.

Coaching the non-athletes. Now let me suggest that we must not overlook the boy and girl non-athletes in our wards and branches. There are many things they can do to assist: they can help to manage the team, they can become timers or scorekeepers, they can become assistant coaches, they can keep statistics on each player, they can become involved in photography. If possible, you should try to involve every young person in a meaningful activity in connection with the team.

Let's also remember that if you have a large ward where there are as many as thirty young men or women, you don't have to have just one great team. You can have a B team and a C team. We have facilities in nearly every stake in the Church such that, given a little creative imagination on the part of the leaders, every boy or girl who wants to play *can* play. For instance, the younger boys generally would make a third team rather than sitting on the bench for two or three years waiting to move up to first string.

Blasting out of the sand traps. We need to be able to teach our youth how to blast out of mental sand traps. Often they need our help to lift them from the very depths of depression and frustration. They need a friend and yet they dare not ask. As coaches we simply have to be so sensitive that we're there when the need arises.

Winston Churchill had been invited to speak to a prep school that he had attended when he was a student. The headmaster told the boys to have their pencils and pads ready and take down whatever he said. When the moment came for him to speak, Churchill, that old warrior, rose to his feet and spoke these words: "Never give in. Never give in. Never, never, never, never, never give in." Then he sat down.

In the proper setting can you see what that would do to a young person?

"The winner never quits, the quitter never wins," I recall someone saying. Someone else has said, "The man who won't be beaten, *can't* be beaten." Seek out motivational mottoes, slogans, etc., and pass them on to the young players to be committed to memory. Recalled in time of need, they can infuse new strength into a weary mind and body.

Teach them "hustle," determination. Hustle can be developed like any other habit. We need to get our charges to run, to hurry, to move aggressively through the game and through life. And every boy and girl who has hustle and determination will also begin to develop drive, the will to win, the urge to be a success.

Some excellent get-up-and-move talk for coaches is found in Jerry Kramer's fine book, *Instant Replay,* in which he relates his experiences in working with Vince Lombardi, the legendary coach of the Green Bay Packers.

Kramer recalls Lombardi's pep-talk preceding one of the games: "This is a game of abandon," Lombardi was telling his backs, "and you run with complete abandon. . . . Nothing, not a tank, not a wall, not a dozen men, can stop you from getting across that goal line.[1]

On another occasion Lombardi told his men, "Winning is not a sometime thing here. It is an all-the-time thing. You don't win once in a while, you don't do things right once in a while, you do them right all the time."[2]

Perhaps the ultimate expression in optimism comes from author Kramer in this recollection:

> The Browns were really laying for us tonight, and they jumped out in front by two touchdowns, 14-0. Some people thought we were in trouble, but we knew we were going to win. We go into every game knowing we're going to win. And we always do. We never lose a game. Sometimes, of course, the clock runs out while the other team still has more points than us, but we know that the game isn't really over, that if we kept playing we'd end up ahead. From our point of view we haven't lost a game in years.[3]

---

[1]From *Instant Replay,* by Jerry Kramer. Copyright © 1968 by Jerry Kramer and Dick Schapp. Reprinted by arrangement with The New American Library, Inc., New York, New York.
[2]*Ibid.*
[3]*Ibid.*

Go easy on the discipline. The time for discipline is during practice. Many of our fine young players get butterflies before a game. They go into a game and they drop a ball or two and immediately some coaches pull them out and have them sit on the bench for the rest of the game.

The wise coach may call a time out, settle the player down, and then let him go in and perform. I do not believe it is good judgment ever to pull a player out of a game right after he has made a mistake. If he has made several mistakes and you feel a need to pull him out, wait until he does something fairly good, or pull him out when it's unnoticeable. It's humiliating enough to make the mistake, and every young man or young woman knows when he or she has made one. Must it be so publicized that everyone in the stands is embarrassed for them?

Teach parents' sportsmanship, too. This chapter would not be complete if we didn't say something about *parents'* sportsmanship. Parents must be taught that sportsmanship is vital on their part, and if a coach sees that the parents in his ward are out of line it would be well next Sunday in priesthood meeting and Sunday School if the bishop stood up and said something about the need of good parents' sportsmanship.

I recall going to a Primary softball game one day and I'll never forget a big, loud, deep-voiced father calling out to a boy eleven years old who was pitching for the opposing team. "Kill the pitcher! Kill the pitcher!" the father kept yelling. I wonder if he realized how ridiculous this sounded to everyone else. The parents of the poor young pitcher were offended, and someone finally had to go and tell this unwise parent how to act at a Church softball game.

What is coaching in our great Church athletic program? It is nothing more, nothing less, than developing boys and girls into adulthood. Putting it another way, it is developing young men and young women to be good citizens; teaching them principles of patriotism, love for God and country, love for physical conditioning. It is nothing more nor less than assisting God in bringing salvation to every young person who participates in Church athletics.

The following expression, taken from a stake priesthood leadership meeting publication, is headed

COACHES NEVER LOSE

A team can lose.
Any team can lose.
But in a sense
A very real sense
A coach never loses.

For the job of a coach
Is over and finished
Once the starting whistle
Blows.
He knows
He's won or lost
Before play starts.

For a coach has two tasks.
The *minor* one is to
Teach skills:
To teach a boy how to run faster
Hit harder
Block better
Kick farther
Jump higher.

The second task
The *major* task
Is to make men
Out of boys.

It's to teach an attitude
Of mind.
It's to implant character
And not simply to impart
Skills.
It's to teach boys to
Play fair.
This goes without saying.

It's to teach them
To be humble in victory
And proud in defeat.
This goes without saying.

But more importantly
It's to teach them
To live up to their potential
No matter what this
Potential is.

It's to teach them
To do their best
And never be satisfied
With what they are
But to strive to be
As good as they could be
If they tried harder.

A coach can never make a
Great player
Out of a boy who isn't
Potentially great.
But he can make a great
Competitor out of any
Child.
And miraculously
He can make a man
Out of a boy.

For a coach
The final score doesn't read:
So many points for my team
So many points for theirs.
Instead it reads:
So many men
Out of so many boys.

And this is a score that
Is never published.
And this is the score
That he reads to himself
And in which he finds
His real joy
When the last game is over.

God bless those who work with our youth in sports and athletics, for they truly have a God-given stewardship — and the opportunity to raise up the greatest generation in the history of the world. Theirs will be a mighty contribution.

10
THE GENTLE
STEWARDSHIP

*Every Latter-day Saint girl, woman, wife and
mother needs to place her hand in the strong
hand of a Melchizedek Priesthood holder and
be unafraid.*

It was a full two weeks before Valentine's Day, but our
Jill, aged seven, was already well along on her preparations.
I came home from work and found a paper sack with a heart
and a valentine verse taped to my door. She had also prepared
one for her mother and one for each of the boys, and had also
put one on her own door. Each night for the next two weeks
I would come home and find she'd made another valentine and
put it in the special sack on my door. I thought how special,
how sweet it was for her to do such a thing at her young age.

About two days before Valentine's Day, my wife startled
me. "You six men in this house are all alike. Every night Jill
makes a valentine for each one of you. Each night and each
morning she checks her valentine sack to see if anyone has
put a valentine in it — and no one has!"

I've never felt more like an ungrateful pup than I did
that night. I sat down at the kitchen table and made about
twenty homemade valentines and took them up and put them

in the sack on Jill's door. In a few minutes she came skipping down the stairs, overflowing with joy — she'd just found her valentines.

Such is the joy of having a girl in the family — especially when you realize that the first five children who blessed our home were boys. We were, of course, grateful beyond measure that the Lord would entrust to our care future priesthood holders and missionaries. In my inexperience, I thought, "What can be better than boys?" When our sixth child came along, Merlene asked the doctor if she could tell me the news. He agreed, so I waited for what seemed an eternity, and then they finally wheeled her out of the delivery room. When I ran to her she cried and said, "Honey, it's — a little girl." I wept sweet, sweet tears. The doctor had tears in his eyes, as did the four interns.

With Jill's coming, I discovered the one thing that could add more joy to our home. We were so grateful for this precious little angel that we named her Jill and called her our "An-Jill." During the first months after she was born, when I would be in a distant city I would climb into my motel bed at night and find myself worrying about that precious little soul. I would think, "I need to get home to protect her!" She awakened emotions and feelings I didn't know existed. It seemed I was always concerned about that tender little soul. Jill has added a dimension to our home that was missing before.

The boys in the family have worshipped her. When our oldest son was called on a mission she was excited, though only aged four at the time. The day after we put him on the plane she asked when he was coming home. I told her not for two years. "How long is two years?" she asked, and I tried to explain, but she couldn't comprehend. Each night she would ask, "When is Ron coming home?" When he called at Christmas, she heard his voice and couldn't even speak. The tears streamed down her cheeks, and finally when he finished talking to her she said, "Please hurry home, Ron. I miss you and I love you." When our second boy was called on a mission she didn't want him to go. The same was true with our third son, Joe, when he left on his mission.

I believe I am beginning to understand a little more about girls and young women.

I remember coming home from the office one day about 7:00 P.M. Merlene was just walking out to teach a Laurel class. She said, "Jill isn't feeling well — stay close to her." So Jill and I stayed home together. I read to her, then I watched a TV show with her for half an hour. After that we played a game or two and finally, about 9:30, I said, "Sweetheart, how are you feeling?"

"I don't feel very well, Daddy, and Mother told me if I didn't feel better I could ask you for a blessing. Will you give me a blessing?"

I said, "Certainly, sweetheart." I went to my room, changed into my suit, white shirt and tie, then went over to her bed. She sat on the edge of the bed and I gave her a blessing. Then I went back into the closet, took off my white shirt and the tie and suit, and got ready for bed.

Do you think she will ever forget that? I doubt it. She may forget the blessing, but she will never forget that I respected my priesthood and her enough to dress appropriately for that occasion. As priesthood holders we owe a proper and righteous exercising of our priesthood powers to our daughters, wives and mothers.

I once read Charlotte Brontë's book *Jane Eyre,* claimed by some readers to be partly her actual autobiography. She tells how Jane Eyre lost both parents and then was sent away to a well-to-do aunt who despised her, could hardly tolerate her. From there she was sent to a girl's poorhouse school, where she spent the next eight years. She had no friends, no one who cared, except Helen Burns, a remarkable girl two or three years older than Jane. Because Helen was so well-adjusted, she helped Jane greatly. Jane leaned on her and loved her dearly.

When a plague of typhus swept through the school, forty-five girls contracted the dread disease and many died. Jane was forbidden to see Helen for several weeks. Finally, in desperation late one night, wanting to visit and minister to Helen, ten-year-old Jane climbed out of bed. She made her way to Helen's room and found her sleeping. The night nurse who sat by her bed was dozing soundly. Jane is speaking as we pick up the story:

"Helen?" I whispered softly; "are you awake?"

She stirred herself, put back the curtain, and I saw her face, pale, wasted, but quite composed: she looked so little changed that my fear was instantly dissipated.

"Can it be you, Jane?" she asked in her own gentle voice.

"Oh!" I thought, "she is not going to die; they are mistaken: she could not speak and look so calmly if she were."

I got on to her crib and kissed her; her forehead was cold, and her cheek both cold and thin, and so were her hand and wrist; but she smiled as of old.

"Why are you come here, Jane: It is past eleven o'clock: I heard it strike some minutes since."

"I came to see you, Helen: I heard you were very ill, and I could not sleep till I had spoken to you."

"You came to bid me good-bye, then: you are just in time, probably."

"Are you going somewhere, Helen? Are you going home?"

"Yes; to my long home — my last home."

"No, no, Helen!" I stopped, distressed. While I tried to devour my tears, a fit of coughing seized Helen; it did not, however, wake the nurse; when it was over, she lay some minutes exhausted; then she whispered:

"Jane, your little feet are bare; lie down and cover yourself with my quilt."

I did so. . . . After a long silence, she resumed; still whispering —

"I am very happy, Jane; and when you hear that I am dead you must be sure and not grieve: there is nothing to grieve about. We all must die one day, and the illness which is removing me is not painful; it is gentle and gradual: my mind is at rest. I leave no one to regret me much: I have only a father; and he is lately married, and will not miss me. By dying young, I shall escape great sufferings. I had not qualities or talents to make my way very well in the world; I should have been continually at fault."

"But where are you going to, Helen? Can you see? Do you know?"

"I believe; I have faith: I am going to God."

"Where is God? What is God?"

"My Maker and yours, who will never destroy what he created. I rely implicitly on his power, and confide wholly in his goodness: I count the hours till that eventful one arrives which shall restore me to him, reveal him to me."

"You are sure, then, Helen, that there is such a place as heaven; and that our souls can get to it when we die?"

"I am sure there is a future state; I believe God is good; I can resign my immortal part to him without any misgiving. God is my father; God is my friend: I love him; I believe he loves me."

"And shall I see you again, Helen, when I die?"

"You will come to the same region of happiness: be received by the same mighty, universal Parent, no doubt, dear Jane."

Again I questioned; but this time only in thought. "Where is that region? Does it exist?" . . . Presently she said in the sweetest tone —

"How comfortable I am! That last fit of coughing has tired me a little: I feel as if I could sleep: but don't leave me, Jane . . ."

"I'll stay with you, dear Helen." . . .

When I awoke it was day; an unusual movement roused me; I looked up; I was in somebody's arms; the nurse held me; she was carrying me through the passage back to the dormitory. I was not reprimanded for leaving my bed; people had something else to think about: no explanation was afforded then to my many questions; but a day or two afterwards I learned that Miss Temple, on returning to her own room at dawn, had found me laid in a little crib, my face against Helen Burns's shoulder, my arms round her neck. I was asleep, and Helen was — dead.

The gentle tenderness of a little girl — the gentle love expressed by a woman at *any* age — is a wonder. A story told me by a choice friend brought this thought even closer to home:

When he was five and his sister was three, their parents were divorced. Neither parent wanted the children. They were sent to live in a children's Christian orphanage, where the dormitories for the girls were separate and well apart from those of the boys. Immediately on their arrival the boy and his little sister were separated. They protested and she cried — but to no avail.

For the next several days the little girl whimpered and cried for her brother. She clung fiercely to her rag doll which she had brought with her. Finally the matron took away her doll and said she would not give it back until she stopped crying. That night this little soul, unobserved, slipped quietly out into the night and — I suppose from instinct alone — found her way to the other dormitory and found her brother. He sat and held her on his lap. She was comforted and contented now, wrapped in the arms of her five-year-old brother.

It wasn't long before the matron missed the child and, after a thorough search, located her with her brother. They pulled the little girl from his young arms and took her back to her dormitory. He never saw her again after that.

One wonders how the heart can endure such pain without breaking.

Later this good brother joined the Church and gained a strength from the knowledge we have of a kind and loving Savior.

Girls respond to love; they need security and tenderness, not harshness, contention, and uncouth actions and language.

Victor Hugo's *Les Miserables,* which to me is the greatest piece of literature outside of the standard works, dramatically symbolizes the need of girls for strength greater than their own.

Hugo describes a moving experience of Fantine's illegitimate daughter Cosette. Fantine wants her eight-year-old daughter to have something better than she had, so she finds a family that, on the surface, looks good and wholesome but who are actually nothing more than a den of the worst kind of vipers. She contracts to have them care for her daughter. They treat her much as Cinderella was treated: they give her no toys, they don't allow her to play, they abuse her, they work her like a servant.

The wicked Thénardiess, her keeper, writes to Fantine and tell her that Cosette is dying and they must have fifty francs to care for her — a lie. Fantine does not have the fifty francs. She goes out into the street and finally passes a man who is buying hair. He sees her beautiful hair which falls in shiny locks to her waist. He offers her fifty francs, and after much mental struggle she sells her hair and sends the demon the money. It comes so easily that the Thénardiers (the man and his wife) write again. To make the story short, she now has to sell her two beautiful white front teeth to save her daughter's life. She sends the money. They demand more. Finally she sells herself, and then becomes ill, and dies. Before she dies she extracts from Jean Valjean a promise to go and get Cosette and care for her. Jean Valjean makes his way to the distant city.

The Thénardiers sat late one night. One of the guests at their inn wanted water for his horse. There was none. The Thénardiers saw the lark "Cosette" playing under the staircase where she slept at night on a mat. It was after 11:00 P.M. Madame Thénardier demanded that Cosette go after the water, which was a considerable distance from the home. The spring was beyond the village lights, out into the dark woods. She was forbidden to take a lantern.

Victor Hugo describes this scene in a way that is unforgettable. He tells of her terror of the night and of the Thénardiers, the latter furnishing the greater fear.

She leaves the village lights and runs with wild-eyed fear to the spring, hardly daring to stop. She fills the bucket and begins her journey back to Montfermeil. Here we pick up the pitiful plight of Cosette in the dark woods as described by Victor Hugo.

Then, by a sort of instinct, to get out of this singular state, which she did not understand, but which terrified her, she began to count aloud, one, two, three, four, up to ten, and when she had finished, she began again. This restored her to a real perception of things about her. Her hands, which she had wet in drawing the water, felt cold. She arose. Her fear had returned, a natural and insurmountable fear. She had only one thought, to fly; to fly with all her might, across woods, across fields, to houses, to windows, to lighted candles. Her eyes fell upon the bucket that was before her. Such was the dread with which the Thénardiess inspired her, that she did not dare to go without the bucket of water. She grasped the handle with both hands. She could hardly lift the bucket.

She went a dozen steps in this manner, but the bucket was full, it was heavy, she was compelled to rest it on the ground. She breathed an instant, then grasped the handle again, and walked on, this time a little longer. But she had to stop again. After resting a few seconds, she started on. She walked bending forward, her head down, like an old woman: the weight of the bucket strained and stiffened her thin arms. The iron handle was numbing and freezing her little wet hands; from time to time she had to stop, and every time she stopped, the cold water that splashed from the bucket fell upon her naked knees. This took place in the depth of a wood, at night, in the winter, far from all human sight; it was a child of eight years; there was none but God at that moment who saw this sad thing.

And undoubtedly her mother, alas!

For there are things which open the eyes of the dead in their grave.

She breathed with a kind of mournful rattle; sobs choked her, but she did not dare to weep; so fearful was she of the Thénardiess, even at a distance. She always imagined that the Thénardiess was near.

However, she could not make much headway in this manner, and was getting along very slowly. She tried hard to shorten her resting spells, and to walk as far as possible between them. She remembered with anguish that it would take her more than an hour to return to Montfermeil thus, and that the Thénardiess would beat her. This anguish added to her dismay at being alone in the woods at night. She was worn out with fatigue, and was not yet out of the forest. Arriving near an old chestnut tree which she knew, she made a last halt, longer than the others, to get well rested; then she gathered all her strength, took up the bucket again, and began to walk on courageously, meanwhile the poor little despairing thing could not help crying: "Oh! my God! my God!"

At that moment she felt all at once that the weight of the bucket was gone. A hand, which seemed enormous to her, had just caught the handle, and was carrying it easily. She raised her head. A large dark form, straight and erect, was walking beside her in the gloom. It was a man who had come up behind her, and whom she had not heard. This man, without saying a word, had grasped the handle of the bucket she was carrying.

There are instincts for all the crises of life.

The child was not afraid.

The stranger, of course, was Jean Valjean.

The "gentle" stewardship is awesome in its implications, but it is not really an exclusive responsibility of the priesthood. Across the Church it is shared by wonderful mothers, by Sunday School teachers, by Primary teachers, and to a very significant degree by officers and teachers in our Young Women's organization.

Ardeth Kapp, one of the great women of the Church, recalls an incident involving the basic needs of girls:

> I had a great experience one time in teaching a group of young girls in the school system. A little girl came into my class at the beginning of the year and her first comment was, "I don't want to be in your class." I felt rather insecure as a new teacher and I thought: "I don't blame you. I don't want to be here either." I said, "Where would you like to be, Connie?" And she said, "I want to be in Miss Bingham's class." And I thought of Miss Bingham, who was cuter and younger and more fun, and had the prettiest room in the school (my room looked kind of comical because I had spent hours there to prepare it).
>
> But Connie was assigned to my room. So I tried to work with her and to understand her. I noticed that her fingernails were bitten halfway down. Each time she would say, "I don't want to come to class," I gave her all the attention I could. I practiced all the principles I knew. I extended love, I tried to communicate, I found out what she was interested in. We started building a relationship and I was feeling pretty good. And then one day we were having a creative writing assignment in an English class and Connie came up to me and said, "Here's my assignment. I would like you to read it." I said, "Just put it in the file and I'll read it after class." "No," she said, "Please read it right now."
>
> So I picked it up and it said: "I hate you. You are ugly. You wear funny shoes." (By the way, when you are a teacher and you're running around, you don't always wear the nicest-looking kinds of shoes.) It also said, "You have hair on your arms." And

I remember looking down and feeling shocked and thinking, "Sure enough." And she had written, "And your hair's a mess." I had been out to recess playing tetherball with the girls and it probably was.

My first reaction was, "You little rascal, after all I've done for you! What kind of gratitude is that?" Then something in my heart said: "Wait. Try to understand this child." So with the kind help of an inner spirit I looked at that paper and said, "Connie, your writing is really improving. I am proud of you." I went on: "You've even indented a paragraph. Now, maybe you would like to put a margin on the page and put it in the file tonight and I'll talk about it with you tomorrow."

She just stood there and looked at me as if to say, "Well, aren't you going to scold me, or aren't you going to say anything?"

I just looked at her, my eyes never wavering, and she went back to her seat. I kind of lost track of her during the day, but at the end of the day I could hardly wait to see what she had done with her paper.

When I took the paper out of the file that night it said: "Dear Mrs. Kapp, I love you. You are the only friend I have. I know you love me."

The Presiding Bishopric has been given the stewardship — by the Lord through his holy prophet — for all the Aaronic Priesthood-age young men and for all the young women of the Church. I am grateful to wonderful sisters like Ardeth Kapp, to the ward bishoprics and branch presidencies which have stewardship over the young women of their wards and to the Young Women's presidents who have been called to preside directly over the young women of the wards and branches. The greatest effort — an effort that translates directly into love and service — must be made on the part of all of us who hold stewardships over the young women of the Church.

One wonders how we can ever face a compassionate and loving God who fully understands the needs and motives of this wonderful generation of his handmaidens. If we fail to make every effort to save our wonderful young women, we will be far more cruel than the matron who came and tore the three-year-old child from her brother's arms. She caused them to suffer mentally, but we may well cause them to suffer spiritually — for all eternity.

As parents in our homes, priesthood holders, and women in youth leadership positions, we must lead this generation of wonderful young women in righteousness and in love. We must not fail, for there are too many of the Lord's choice daughters and handmaidens whose eternal welfare is at stake. They will follow where we lead in righteousness. They will honor and sustain us. They will be devoted and faithful in their callings. But we must exercise righteousness and give a total commitment in fulfilling our oaths and covenants and our responsibilities of leadership.

If we do this we will have the young women of the Church respond to us as Ruth did to Naomi:

> Intreat me not to leave thee, or to return from following after thee: for whither thou goest, I will go; and where thou lodgest, I will lodge: thy people shall be my people, and thy God my God. (Ruth 1:16.)

Obtaining such a response must be our hope and our firm goal.

11
YOUTH IN
TRANSGRESSION

Every young person must be helped to under-
stand the seriousness of a major transgression.
And every young person deserves a thorough,
searching interview by a wise judge in order
either to declare his worthiness or to determine
what action may be required for him to receive
full forgiveness from the Lord.

I have a close friend who served for many years as a
bishop. He recalls the story of Bob and Barbara (not their
real names) who were engaged to be married — "one-hundred percenters" he called them, their parents on both sides
being quality members of the Church. The bishop remembered what a wonderful experience it was to watch them
as they dated and courted — this lovely young couple totally
active in the Church, involved fully in every way.

Shortly before their marriage they made an appointment
to see him. As he sat behind the desk and this couple came
into his office, he moved out from behind the desk, sat beside
them, and said, "I know why you're here — you've come to
get a temple recommend, haven't you?"

"My heart just leaped," he recalled, "at the prospect of
issuing them temple recommends. But that's not what hap-

pened. Instead, Bob dropped his head and Barbara began to weep silently. Bob finally looked up and said, 'No, bishop, that's not why we're here. I wish with all my heart it were, but it's not. We've been immorally involved with each other, and now Barbara is expecting and we don't know what to do.' "

The bishop said later: "If you'd hit me with a sledge-hammer it couldn't have hurt any more. These two wonderful young people — these 'one-hundred percenters' — were sitting before me now, confessing to having violated the moral code." The good bishop wept with them, and then the three of them talked about forgiveness. They all knelt down together and the bishop offered a prayer, pleading with the Lord to show him how they might counsel together to help this couple to somehow return to full fellowship and activity in the Church.

As he counseled with them, a course of action was decided upon. The couple willingly agreed to carry out the specifics of this course — they were willing to do anything. They painfully explained the situation to their parents, they set a tentative date for marriage at the home of the bride-to-be, and the wedding was performed by the bishop. Bob and Barbara moved into a little apartment within the ward, and shortly thereafter their first child came along.

A little over a year later, because this couple had done everything the bishop had asked them to do — had repented in every way, had accepted every assignment, had paid their tithes and offerings, had volunteered to serve on the welfare farm, and so on — the bishop recommended that Bob be ordained an elder. A short time later, Bob and Barbara went to the temple and were sealed to each other. Their first child was sealed to them, and within a year or so another child came along.

Approximately five years after their marriage, a rather special fast and testimony meeting took place in the ward. The bishop recalls the sweet influence in that meeting, the overwhelming outpouring of the Lord's Spirit. Following the

closing prayer no one moved. Everyone remained in their
seats — no one wanted to leave. After a while one or two
got up, then a few more, and finally everyone began to move
slowly out of the chapel. One by one they came by, shaking
hands with the bishop. Finally, at the end of the line, there
stood Barbara. "Bishop," she said, "I don't know how to
thank you for what you've done for Bob and me."

"Well, what have I done for you kids?" the bishop responded. "You're the best young couple in the ward; I've
done very little to help you — you've always been one-hundred percenters."

"Well, don't you remember the problem we had, Bishop?"

And he replied, "What is in the past is closed, and now
we look to the future; and the future is spotless."

The Lord has promised those who truly repent that he
will remember their sins no more. And if *he* remembers them
no more, of course the Lord's servants should remember them
no more. I believe a sweet, kind, loving Heavenly Father will
not only forget Bob and Barbara's transgression but will also
take it from the mind of the bishop.

On the other hand, nonrepentant transgressions remain
in the concerned mind of the bishop or stake president.

Shortly after I had been called to the Presiding Bishopric,
an Arizona stake president told me he had a young missionary
candidate who needed to be interviewed for worthiness. I
asked the stake president if the bishop had recommended this
young man without reservation. He said that he had. I asked
the stake president if he recommended him to me and he said
he thought he could.

As I invited the young man into my office, after his
having been cleared by his bishop and stake president, I said
to him: "Apparently there has been a major transgression
in your life. That's why I am involved in this interview.
Would you mind being very frank and open and telling me
what that transgression was?"

With head held high and in a haughty manner he responded, "There isn't *anything* I haven't done."

I responded: "Well, then, let's be more specific. Have you been involved in fornication?"

Very sarcastically, he said, "I told you I've done *everything.*"

I asked, "Was it a single experience, or did it happen with more than one girl and more than once?"

And he said again, sarcastically, "Many girls and so many times I could not number them."

I said, "I would to God your transgression was not so serious."

"Well, it is," he replied.

"How about drugs?"

"I told you I've done *everything.*"

Then I said, "What makes you think you're going on a mission?"

"Because I have repented," he replied. "I haven't done any of these things for a year. I know I'm going on a mission because my patriarchal blessing says I'm going on a mission. I've been ordained an elder, I've lived the way I should this past year, and I know that I'm going on a mission."

I looked at the young man sitting across the desk: twenty-one years old, laughing, sarcastic, haughty, with an attitude far removed from sincere repentance. And I said to him: "My dear young friend, I'm sorry to tell you this, but you are *not* going on a mission. Do you suppose we could send you out with your braggadocio attitude about this past life of yours, boasting of your escapades? Do you think we could send you out with the fine, clean young men who have never violated the moral code, who have kept their lives clean and pure and worthy so that they might go on missions?"

I repeated: "You're not going on a mission. In fact," I said, "you shouldn't have been ordained an elder and you really should have been tried for your membership in the Church."

"What you have committed is a series of monumental transgressions," I continued. "You haven't repented; you've just stopped doing something. Someday, after you have been to Gethsemane and back, you'll understand what true repentance is."

At this the young man started to cry. He cried for about five minutes, and during that time I didn't say a word. (By the way, let me suggest that there are times during an interview when it would be inappropriate to say anything — when we should just wait, and listen, and watch, and let the person do some soul-searching and thinking.) I just sat and waited as this young man cried.

Finally he looked up and said, "I guess I haven't cried like that since I was five years old."

I told him: "If you had cried like that the first time you were tempted to violate the moral code, you may well have been going on a mission today. Now, I'm sorry, I hate to be the one to keep you from realizing your goal. I know it will be hard to go back to your friends and tell them you are not going on a mission.

"After you've been to Gethsemane," I continued, "you'll understand what I mean when I say that every person who commits a major transgression must also go to Gethsemane and back before he is forgiven."

The young man left the office, and I'm sure he wasn't very pleased; I had stood in his way and kept him from going on a mission.

About six months later, I was down in Arizona speaking at the institute at Tempe. After my talk many of the institute members came down the aisles to shake hands. As I looked up I saw this young man — the nonrepentant transgressor — coming down the aisle toward me, and at that moment the details of my interview with him came back through my mind.

I recalled his braggadocio attitude, his sarcasm, his haughtiness.

I reached down to shake hands with him, and as he looked up at me I could see that something wonderful had taken place in his life. Tears streamed down his cheeks. An almost holy glow came from his countenance. I said to him, "You've been there, haven't you?"

And through tears he said, "Yes, Bishop Featherstone, I've been to Gethsemane and back."

"I know," I said. "It shows in your face. I believe now that the Lord has forgiven you."

He responded: "I'm more grateful to you than you'll ever know for not letting me go on a mission. It would have been a great disservice to me. Thanks for helping me."

What a tragedy it would have been to let this young man go on a mission! Can you imagine the influence he would have had, with his previous attitude, going out across the mission field, being exposed to one young man after another, never having truly repented, boasting about all of those things he had done in his past? He could not have been a cleansed vessel. Conceivably, he could have even affected other missionaries adversely. The situation recalls the words of President J. Reuben Clark, Jr.: "It is one thing to forgive a man, and another thing to place him on a pedestal." (Quoted by President Harold B. Lee to the Presiding Bishopric in their meeting with the First Presidency.)

In the cases of the "one-hundred percenter" young couple and the nonrepentant transgressor, I believe both the couple and (later) the young man were forgiven. The great "miracle of forgiveness" takes place when we follow the pattern that the Lord has required. In both cases the participants truly repented and were forgiven. That is the point at which the bishop as the common judge in Israel — or the stake president functioning in that capacity — may make the necessary judgment and bring the transgressors back into full activity, remembering their sins no more.

Sometimes the overcoming of transgression requires far more than a stern interview or a word of counsel. It may require an ongoing program of "direct aid," as the bishop or even the stake president works with a youth over weeks, months, even years.

While I was stake president a young man who had been involved in transgression came to visit me. His bishop had interviewed him several times, and each time the young man had promised he would cease his immoral conduct with his girl friend. Then the bishop would call him in again to interview him, only to find that the young man had not ceased at all. The bishop had interviewed him several times and finally, not knowing what to do, had turned him over to me.

In my interview with this young man I was brutally frank. I said: "You have been given the opportunity to repent of your transgression. You have not taken that opportunity and now, my dear young friend, functioning as one of the Lord's common judges in Israel I tell you that you may well suppose that you will be excommunicated from the Church."

The young man was shocked. He couldn't believe what he was hearing. He had known of others who had violated the code and slipped by, and now here he was, being called in and threatened with excommunication. We should always interview in the spirit of section 121 of the Doctrine and Covenants — "Reproving betimes with sharpness, when moved upon by the Holy Ghost; and then showing forth afterwards an increase in love toward him whom thou hast reproved" — and I did so on this occasion. Nevertheless, it was the shock and impact of that interview that led this young man to do some great soul-searching.

I interviewed him regularly and found that his attitude changed, that he made adjustments so that he was not led into this temptation any more. He and his girl friend set up a wedding date and he began to prepare himself for a temple marriage. In due course, after his repentance was complete, he was brought back into full fellowship in the Church.

The intent is, of course, that we help the youth not to get that deep into sin rather than have to assist them out of it. With this in mind, and because of the absolute need for bishops to focus clearly on the realities of youth transgressions and to follow through in helping the youth over their serious problems, the worthiness interview and all subsequent contacts are enormously important.

As youth prepare for an interview with the bishop, they should be invited to come dressed appropriately. A young man ought to be attired in a dress shirt and in slacks and a sport coat or a suit. A young woman should be dressed modestly and appropriately.

An opening prayer should be offered, and at the close of the interview the bishop may want to kneel with the young person and give him (or her) a special blessing. Alternatively he may feel impressed to simply ask the young person if he would like a special blessing. If he receives an affirmative response, the bishop may walk over and place his hands upon the head of the young person and, being guided by the Spirit, pronounce a blessing that will give that youth more strength, more power and courage to meet the temptations and trials ahead.

In the interview, bishops need to remember that the youth we work with come from all kinds of backgrounds. Some come from broken homes, or from homes where there is no love, or from homes characterized by jealousy and bitterness in the family, or from homes where there is unfaithfulness between the parents. Some come from homes where parents have been disciplined, have been excommunicated from the Church. Some come from homes where there is intense love, where the gospel is continuously practiced. Some come from homes where parents are bishops or stake presidents or other prominent Church leaders.

I believe that as we focus on the individual, as we get to know enough about the young person's past, we can truly reflect upon each as a person of worth, as a son or daughter of God. Then, and only then, can we make a real contribution as leaders in assisting youth in this area of transgression.

In greeting the young men and young women, the bishop ought to be sincerely warm and interested. He should let them feel that he has all the time they need. If he has only fifteen minutes, he must not let them feel the pressure of time he feels. He should provide a climate for warmth and closeness without ever doing anything that could be misconstrued by an imaginative youth; that is, being careful to follow all the rules of propriety when interviewing.

As to the approach, the bishop should first talk with the person for a few minutes about his success in school and in Church, about his achievements, about his parents, his seminary teacher, the basketball coach, and so on. When the young person is loosened up in this way he will speak freely and easily with the bishop. After he has been warmed up, an approach might be: "Now, my dear young brother (or sister), I've called you into this special interview and I want you to be totally frank and honest with me. The Lord has given to his bishop the authority to conduct such interviews as the common judge of the people. As you speak honestly and forthrightly, the sweet spirit of peace will come into my heart; I will know you are telling the truth. If not, the spirit will not be at peace; I won't be able to tell you why, but I will just know there is something wrong in the interview. So please speak honestly and openly, and with total frankness."

With that introduction, the question might now come, "My dear friend, are you living the Word of Wisdom?" Be specific in this. Ask, "Tea?" Let him respond. "Coffee?" Again let him respond. "Liquor? Beer?" Include some of the specific temptations with which a young person might be faced. "Have you been involved with cigarettes? with drugs?" Watch very carefully the eyes of the young person. Depend heavily upon the Spirit of the Lord, and if the Spirit whispers peace, go on to the next part of the interview. If not, keep probing until you find out what the problem has been.

There are other questions that need to be asked, much as in a temple recommend interview. "Do you sustain the bishop? your stake president? the General Authorities of the Church?" Explain to them what it means to sustain a leader, namely, being willing to accept whatever he calls us to do, whatever assignment he may ask us to perform.

"Now, are you keeping the Sabbath day holy?" With our young people, we need to be understanding; we can't expect them to do all that we older folks would do on Sunday as regards visiting the sick, reading the scriptures all day long, being involved in total rest. We ought to help them set a standard. For example, "What percentage of the time do you attend priesthood meeting, Sunday School, sacrament meeting?

If they are doing all these things, I would suggest asking questions on a higher order of faithfulness, such as visiting the widows or reading the scriptures. But we should not be overly critical if they aren't doing all these things; after all, learning to be the kind of Latter-day Saint the Lord expects us to be is a lifetime project.

There may be many other questions the bishop will ask the young person, such as those on tithing, seminary attendance, and other subjects, but he has been working up to the point where he can talk about the moral code. As he gets to this delicate area, he may ask the question in this way: "Are you morally clean?" (Almost always the answer is yes.) Unfortunately, this is as much detail as some of our bishops go into in interviewing the youth. But this is not sufficient. Our young people need to have the privilege of being interviewed so that we can help them to solve their serious problems.

Some of our young people are involved in petting, and I would simply ask them the direct question, "Are you involved in petting?" It may be necessary to define the term. Our youth need to know that this is a serious transgression. We need to teach them that the fact that others indulge in this sin is no excuse for an LDS youth to do so.

Some of our young people, especially those of college age, will be involved in immoral activities in which they will do everything except actually commit fornication. Hence, if the bishop asks them, "Have you ever committed fornication?" they can say no, and yet they may have done everything except actually perform the act. These people must be helped, and the interview can be extremely useful to this end.

As the bishop questions in detail, he should remember always to be aware of the age of the young person and his possible exposure to some of these problems. We do not question a twenty-year-old youth as we do a thirteen-year-old, or vice versa. On the other hand, we need to be aware of those who, although fairly youthful (perhaps thirteen-fifteen), have a manner and attitude which could lead to this type of transgression. We should not hesitate to ask penetrating and probing questions appropriate to the young person's age and circumstances.

There is another sexual-related personal problem which besets many young men and some young women. A thoughtful, helpful bishop or parent will question in such a way that the problem will surface. Once we know the problem exists we can outline a program to assist our youth in overcoming that problem. Additionally a bishop or a father would be wise to give a young man or young woman a special blessing with power to overcome temptation. This will mean a great deal more than we would usually imagine.

A few of our bishops feel that this personal problem is not too serious because "everyone does it." This is not true. In the book *The Miracle of Forgiveness* by President Spencer W. Kimball, we find just how serious this transgression is. And I may say that some of our adults, never having been properly interviewed, never achieving an understanding on this matter, go through married life, and even into their mature years, still having serious problems in this area.

As we interview young women, of course, we don't want to offend the delicate sensitivities of those who are so modest that they don't even know some of the terms used in this area, let alone their meanings. Bishops will be able to discern by the Spirit which girls need to be asked certain questions and which do not.

After I had finished speaking at a Young Adult conference, a young woman of about twenty came up and asked me for an interview. She said that she had a particular health problem and wanted a special blessing. I asked, "Is there anything in your life which is not right, which would keep you from receiving the blessing you desire?"

It turned out that she did have a personal problem, a moral problem which she had already discussed with her bishop. With her bishop's approval, I gave her the special blessing she was seeking.

I took time and counseled this young woman. I suggested how she might overcome her problem. As I left her there were tears in her eyes as she said: "I appreciate what you've told me; I'll try to live the way you've suggested. I'll get back to my bishop as you suggested and report to him on how I'm doing."

The young members of the Church deserve this kind of help.

A problem of serious concern is that of homosexuality. We have it in some degree in the Church, though less than outside. It's a serious problem for those involved in it. Bishops have a supplement packet to the Welfare Services Handbook to give guidance and direction on this matter. They also have the resource of professional and Church agencies.

We must be ever aware of such problems, and youth leaders who feel that this problem exists with one of the young people under their charge should immediately go to the bishop and counsel with him. Like heterosexual offenses, homosexuality is a major transgression. It is to be confessed to the bishop before the guilty one can receive forgiveness. There are a few instances in which a young man or woman may be involved once and once only. Frequently, these offenses, as they are confessed, may be quickly forgiven, forgotten, and closed forever.

In overcoming tendencies toward homosexuality, what a boy needs above all else is a father who presents a masculine image. And the boy needs to do some good, hard, vigorous work.

I recall President Harold B. Lee telling of a young man who came to see him because he had tendencies toward homosexuality, although he had never been directly involved. He said that he was being drafted and that he would be asked about such tendencies, and his question to President Lee was, "Should I tell a lie and go into the service, where I'll be confronted with the temptation, or should I tell the truth and become a marked man for the rest of my life?"

This was a serious, perplexing problem. President Lee wisely counseled the young man to tell the draft board that he had this problem, that he had not been directly involved, but that it was a serious temptation and trial to him. The young man did this, and was not accepted into the military service. President Lee then counseled him to go out to Nevada and work on a farm.

The young man complied, and after he had been on the farm for some months, he returned home. As President Lee had hoped, the hard physical work had been good therapy. As he approached President Lee he said that he had met a sweet girl who was also a member of the Church and they were getting married. And he added that his former problem was no longer a concern to him.

For those who have been involved in homosexuality, it is vital that we follow certain courses of action. First we need to find out that the problem exists and help that young person in overcoming it. We need to let him know how serious the problem is — equal to fornication or adultery. We need to let him know that, should he choose not to repent, his Church membership will be in jeopardy, that he may be called before a court of the Church and disciplined.

If he is willing to repent, we should then outline a program and assist him in receiving forgiveness for his major transgressions. Importantly, because homosexuals have been involved with each other in a type of perverted love, it will be necessary for the priesthood leader to expect from either the young man (or young woman) that he or she cease having any kind of contact with the other party, that the relationship be absolutely terminated. "Just being friends" almost never succeeds. Breaking off a homosexual relationship is an extremely difficult thing for the person to do, but it is an inescapable part of repentance.

Such young people must be brought to understand that all of God's children are tempted, and that in many cases it takes a lifetime to develop total self-mastery wherein we control every thought and every action, wherein we put behind us the desire to commit fornication, adultery, or homosexuality. In the words of Paul: "There hath no temptation taken you but such as is common to man: but God is faithful, who will not suffer you to be tempted above that ye are able: but will with the temptation also make a way to escape, that ye may be able to bear it." (1 Corinthians 10:13.) Sometimes, a part of that "way to escape" is a special blessing, given in all humility by the bishop. It can be a powerful influence in overcoming such problems as we have been discussing.

As we interview our young people who have not yet received the Melchizedek Priesthood, who have not yet been on missions or been married in the temple, we should be careful not to be harsh with them if through lack of willpower or of self-mastery they have succumbed to temptation and violated the moral code. We should continue to forgive and work with them, exercising more patience with these members who have had less experience in the Church. After all, their whole life is ahead of them; we should persuade and teach and do all we can to induce in them a desire to repent. Only when they totally rebel and turn away from counsel, when they commit the sin time after time, blatantly and without any desire to repent, should they be called into a Church court.

In an earlier chapter we discussed the tremendous influence for good that a "third-party" leader (a person other than an immediate family member or the bishop) can exercise in a youth relationship. In this connection I recall that some years ago, while I was on my way to a special meeting, a young man phoned me and said, "Brother Featherstone, I know you're just my Sunday School teacher, but I have a problem." He continued: "You know I've been going with this girl for quite a while, and now we're engaged and I'm planning to marry her in the temple. But every evening when I go out with her I'm just not sure I'll come home clean and pure — whether I'll be able and worthy to receive a temple recommend. My wedding date is still about three months off, and I don't know how long I can resist the temptation. Can you please, please help me?"

I remember talking with him for almost forty-five minutes. I counseled him from the very depths of my soul, calling upon Heavenly Father and pleading that I might say the right thing to this young man. I remember working with him over the next two or three months, occasionally just counseling him — not daring to ask if he was morally clean; this was not my prerogative as a Sunday School teacher. I just kept building him up, bringing to our Sunday School lessons things that would strengthen him and others who might be in similar circumstances.

I well recall the day, three or four months later, when this fine young man, still worthy, took his sweetheart to the temple. It's true: Many times our young people are severely tempted.

Youth leaders can often give help by drawing on their past experiences. I recall being with a group of Explorers who took canoes down the Snake River one summer. We decided that we would have a spiritual experience each evening as we floated down the river. I took the first night and tried to provide the young men with a fine spiritual experience as we sat around a fire out in that beautiful Wyoming-Idaho area. I remember turning to one of the leaders and asking him if he would take the next night. After the campfire meeting was over he came to me and said, "I don't know what I would tell them." The next day he was still concerned and he came to me several times. "I just haven't come up with anything yet," he kept saying.

But finally that night, after we had finished dinner and built a fire and sang a few songs around the campfire, I turned the time over to this fine leader. Here was his story:

> Many years ago I used to play on a basketball team — in fact we went all the way to the state tournament. The night of the state tournament, just before the game started, one of the cheerleaders came onto the floor and asked the fellows if they'd like to come over to her house for a party after the game. Thinking more about the game, the fellows didn't give it a second thought — they didn't even respond to her question — but after the game ended and we'd won, one of the team members remembered the invitation. So the whole basketball team — all twelve of them — got together and went over to the girl's house.
>
> We found that the girl's parents were gone over the weekend, and that she had invited exactly twelve girls to her home as well as the team. She soon rolled the rug back and had the stereo going. They turned it up loud, and then the girl who was the hostess went into the kitchen and came out with a carton of cigarettes. She threw a package over to the fellow who was sitting on the end, and she said, "Hey, training's all over. We can smoke tonight."
>
> Well, we were from a Mormon community. I watched the first fellow — he took a cigarette. Then the girl next to him took one. So did the girl next to her. And as the cigarettes got closer and closer to me, it seemed that almost everyone there was taking a cigarette.
>
> It was an embarrassing moment and I didn't know how to handle it.
>
> Finally I thought, "Oh well, it's only one cigarette and I guess I can smoke with them." Anyway, when the cigarettes went to the fellow right next to me, he said, "No, thanks, I don't smoke," and passed them on.

The strength of the friend on my left gave me the courage to do what I really wanted to do all along. I said, "No, thanks," too.

The thing I have wondered through all these years is, what would have happened to me if I had been sitting on *the other side* of my friend?

That is a great story, and it poses the sort of a question that must often be asked. We have great friends in the Church and they can help us to overcome temptation. The youth ought to align themselves with the fine young men and young women who will resist wrong peer pressures; and as bishops and others leaders we ought to encourage those in youth leadership positions to be close friends with those who need such strength in their peer group.

Where *do* we stand, anyway? That's a question our youth should be asking themselves constantly. And it's a question that bishops should be asking them — through the worthiness interview.

As I have already indicated, our young people deserve a thorough and searching interview. If you leaders will look back through your youth, in many cases you will find that you never had the privilege of going through a thorough and searching interview. No one ever asked you about personal problems. No one ever asked you about petting. No one ever asked you about having transgressed the moral laws. And so you perhaps became vulnerable to Satan's temptation, saying, "Why not do it? No one will ask."

But someone *should* ask — the common judge in Israel. The Lord told Alma: "Therefore I say unto you, Go; and whosoever transgresseth against me, him shall ye judge according to the sins which he has committed; and if he confess his sins before thee and me, and repenteth in the sincerity of his heart, him shall ye forgive, and I will forgive him also."

Our young people need to know that they may be forgiven and that the Lord will forgive them also: "Yea, and as often as my people repent will I forgive them their trespasses against me." (Mosiah 26:29-30.)

In verse 31 we read: "And ye shall also forgive one another your trespasses; for verily I say unto you, he that forgiveth not his neighbor's trespasses when he says that he repents, the same hath brought himself under condemnation." This is the vital key to repentance in the lives of our young people as well as the older members.

May God bless you youth leaders to lead our young people in a manner that will bring them to total repentance and forgiveness in his kingdom. More especially, may God bless you who have never violated the moral code, who will be the kind of leaders who help our youth to stand steadfast and walk uprightly before the Lord, to be strong in the faith and never compromise the moral principles of the gospel.

The youth need your example. May you strive to prove worthy of this trust.

12
TOWARD
REWARDING WORK

Because of the great principles of integrity and work taught by the Church, parents and other youth leaders are in a position to develop a generation of youth who will evoke the admiration of the world.

According to legend, the king of a far-off country was suffering from boredom. He proclaimed the need of a game to entertain him, one that would not only supply the excitement any good game should offer but would provide endless variation.

Dutifully his subjects set out to conceive such a game, and month after month people came to him with games of all descriptions. But none of the games satisfied the king; they tended to sameness and were unimaginative.

Then one day a young man came to him with a flat board he had divided into sixty-four equal squares. He had what he called "men" that he moved back and forth on the squares. The name of the game was chess — and it looked interesting enough to try. The king played it one day; then a second day; and on through a week — and a month. He was fascinated! He was in fact so enchanted with the new game that he never tired of it.

To properly reward the game's originator, the king asked what he might desire. The young man thought for a minute and said, "I would like a grain of wheat for the first square, two grains for the second square, four for the third square, and so on through the sixty-four squares."

The king quickly responded: "Surely you want more than that! Let me give you something of *worth*."

"If you'll simply grant me a grain for the first square, then double it each time for the sixty-four squares, that is all I desire," the man replied.

The king sent one of the servants out for a bushel of wheat to pay off the man. But as you have probably already guessed, one bushel was hardly enough, for the payment asked for, a geometric progression based on the sixty-four squares on the board, would have required more than 9,000,-000,000,000,000,000 grains of wheat, or a several-year supply for the whole world. Needless to say, the king was incredulous.

The story has a point that relates directly to the vocational development of our youth: Each time a boy or girl develops a new skill, it multiplies itself countless times over a lifetime in terms of its value to the youth as well as potentially to mankind. It doesn't matter whether that skill is in surgery, in education, or in some particular trade or vocation; the principle is always true: there is a huge return on the investment.

As parents and others leaders of youth, which vocations, which professions should we be encouraging them to pursue? If we can build into our young people not simply a concept of *what* vocation or profession they should go into, but rather *how they should approach* that vocation or profession — with a spirit of achieving excellence, of doing the very best job they can — we will truly be filling our callings as "vocational counselors" in the fullest sense of that term.

A pride in self and in work is what's really important here, and as we teach true excellence we must also teach that the excellence for which we strive must be accompanied by *integrity.* For motivation without integrity and character is shallow. It brings only a false sense of fulfillment.

Speaking on the campus at Stanford University early this century, William James said, "The world is only beginning to see that more than anything else the wealth of a nation is measured in the number of superior men it harbors." This is just as true in the Church. The wealth of our Church is really measured in the number of superior men and women we develop through the teachings of the Savior, through their compliance with his principles and commandments. And of course we can see this kind of wealth represented in virtually all vocations and professions.

I know a great man, Ronald Loveland, who was in a priests quorum I taught. Ronald Loveland was a one-hundred percenter. His dad was a great worker in the plumbing and heating business, and Ronald took up the trade, making good wages and progressing quickly. In the early morning hours before work would start, he taught seminary. Previous to becoming a plumber, while he was on his mission, he was assistant to the mission president and showed a fine ability to get results. Afterwards he applied this same drive and ability to his vocation.

I recall what a great privilege it was to call him to the high council while I was stake president, and then see him called as a bishop. Later I saw this fine young man, then in his early thirties, called into the stake presidency. He was also called to serve in the San Antonio Texas Mission as the mission president. One young man who returned from that mission said, "Ronald Loveland is the greatest man I have ever known in my life."

But what about his being a plumber? How does a vocation like that rate with, say, medicine or law? The answer came as I watched this fine man in a leadership meeting as he gave a teaching demonstration that would have caused the college professors to sit up and take notice. He did a profound job. He communicated. And when his demonstration ended, his message lingered on, branding itself on the hearts of everyone present.

There is great talent in the membership of the Church, and, so long as the proposed occupation is honorable, it matters not whether it is sought among what are called the professions or the trades. What we must teach our youth is this: The Church needs every member, and any man or woman, whether he or she be a carpenter, a plumber, a salesperson, a teacher or a housewife — all can achieve greatness equal to that of the doctor or lawyer, the statesman or diplomat.

We need not recount the vocations of those whom the Savior gathered close to him. We need simply remind our youth that he himself, a carpenter, was also the greatest teacher who ever lived, a man who became the greatest leader, the greatest motivator, the greatest achiever, with the greatest following of any being who ever walked this earth.

Two brothers were in my priests quorum at the same time as Ronald Loveland: Dennis and Lawrence Flake. These young men were raised on a farm. They had to get up early every morning to milk cows and do chores. After school they were very much involved in other jobs around the farm. They were excellent cowboys, though Dennis was somewhat less than a natural athlete. I remember one night after work when we were having softball practice; Dennis was there with us — he played in the field. He loved sports but they just didn't come easy, and as a result he wasn't one of the better players on the team.

Dennis went on a mission; he became an assistant to the mission president in Australia. He returned home and prepared himself to teach in the Church educational system. At time of writing he heads up the Home Study division in the southern states for the seminary program. He lives about as close to the Lord as any human being could possibly live. He is doing the thing that gives him the greatest fulfillment: teaching religious principles to the sons and daughters of God, wherever they may be.

His brother Lawrence is not a whit behind Dennis in terms of his contribution. He too is involved in the Church education system — as supervisor of the institute and seminaries programs for a large area in the East — and is a mighty influence for God. Most of the other brothers in the Flake family are also involved in the seminary or institute program. These men — these ex-farm boys — are making great contributions to the Church. They love the scriptures; they love teaching the principles of the gospel. Surely it would have been folly to try to force these fine young men into sports, farming, or some other pattern or mold that someone else felt would have been best for them. No doubt their father longed for at least one of them to stay on the farm with him. They chose not to do this, and this great father had the wisdom to let his sons do that which would bring them the greatest fulfillment in life.

As parents and leaders of youth we all must have this same trust and confidence in the youth of our generation.

Ofttimes we as adults tend to force our youth into a mold that fits society. We expect every young person to go into a profession, to graduate from a college or university, and in the process we place too much stress on a "higher" education, to the detriment of those who would find gainful, honorable employment in the trades or other vocations.

While some youth desire to and *should* go into professions, and some should go into business administration, other youth should be working with their hands, finding the fulfillment that comes from putting their hearts and souls into that kind of work.

By way of a negative example of misdirection, I recall a friend who was on the track team at the same time I was in high school. He had more natural track and field ability than anyone else in the school. He could sprint, run long-distance, high jump, broad jump, pole vault. He entered the decathlon and took first place in the state. I expected him to go on to college and become a great athlete at college level. But in spite of his great talent, the *desire* was not there. His life became one of dissipation as he destroyed the body with which the Lord had blessed him. Other young men with not nearly his level of talent, out of sheer desire and determination moved forward in athletics and went on to become university all-conference stars in football, track, basketball, and other sports.

In life, *attitude* is far more important than aptitude — some 85 percent of success is attributed to attitude and 15 percent to ability or skills. This statistic has been kicked around for years, and I suspect it is fairly accurate.

I have seen many young men approach the grocery business during the twenty-six years I was engaged in it (I worked in the grocery business from the time I was fifteen until I was called into the Presiding Bishopric). The grocery industry provides great opportunities for part-time work. Many young men and women have worked their way through universities and colleges as checkers and stock clerks and in other positions. Many have gone on to great professions, others have gone into business, and many have stayed in the grocery industry. It has always seemed to me that attitude has played by far the most important role in the success — or lack of success — of these youth. Many who did not have the aptitude to work as physically hard as the grocery business demands pushed themselves to be successful in that business in order to maintain the job while going through school. This is part of life. Achieving success, developing leadership qualities, is not easy. Angela Morgan teaches us that in her poem, "When Nature Wants a Man."

WHEN NATURE WANTS A MAN[1]

When Nature wants to drill a man
And thrill a man
And skill a man,
When Nature wants to mould a man
To play the noblest part;
When she yearns with all her heart
To create so great and bold a man

---

[1]Reprinted by permission of Dodd, Mead and Company, Inc. from *Forward March!* by Angela Morgan. Copyright 1918 by Dodd, Mead and Company, Inc. Copyright renewed 1946.

That all the world shall praise —
Watch her methods, watch her ways!
How she ruthlessly perfects
Whom she royally elects;
How she hammers him and hurts him
And with mighty blows converts him
Into trial shapes of clay which only Nature understands —
While his tortured heart is crying and he lifts beseeching hands! —
How she bends but never breaks
When his good she undertakes. . . .
How she uses whom she chooses
And with every purpose fuses him,
By every art induces him
To try his splendor out —
Nature knows what she's about.

When Nature wants to take a man
And shake a man
And wake a man,
When Nature wants to make a man
To do the Future's will;
When she tries with all her skill
And she yearns with all her soul
To create him large and whole, . . .
With what cunning she prepares him!
How she goads and never spares him!
How she whets him and she frets him
And in poverty begets him. . . .
How she often disappoints
Whom she sacredly anoints,
With what wisdom she will hide him,
Never minding what betide him
Though his genius sob with slighting and his pride may not forget!
Bids him struggle harder yet,
Makes him lonely
So that only
God's high messages shall reach him,
So that she may surely teach him
What the Hierarchy planned.
Though he may not understand,
Gives him passions to command —
How remorselessly she spurs him,
With terrific ardor stirs him,
When she poignantly prefers him!

When Nature wants to name a man
And fame a man
And tame a man;
When Nature wants to shame a man
To do his heavenly best. . . .
When she tries the highest test
That her reckoning may bring —
When she wants a God or king! —
How she reins him and restrains him
So his body scarce contains him,
While she fires him
And inspires him!
Keeps him yearning, ever burning for a tantalizing goal —
Lures and lacerates his soul,
Sets a challenge for his spirit,
Draws it higher when he's near it —
Makes a jungle, that he clear it,
Makes a desert that he fear it,
And subdue it if he can —
So doth Nature make a man.
Then, to test his spirit's wrath
Hurls a mountain in his path —
Puts a bitter choice before him
And relentlessly stands o'er him.
"Climb, or perish!" so she says. . . .
Watch her purpose, watch her ways!

Nature's plan is wondrous kind
Could we understand her mind. . . .
Fools are they who call her blind.
When his feet are torn and bleeding
Yet his spirit mounts unheeding,
All his higher powers speeding,
Blazing newer paths and fine;
When the force that is divine
Leaps to challenge every failure
And his ardor still is sweet
And love and hope are burning in the presence of defeat. . . .
Lo, the crisis! Lo, the shout
That must call the leader out.
When the people need salvation,
Doth he come to lead the nation. . . .
Then doth Nature show her plan,
When the world has found — a man!

There is one great, common ground for all LDS young men and women: *they all can achieve leadership* in the kingdom. Just as my plumber friend became a mission president, so also others of various backgrounds and occupations are great leaders within the Church.

Why? Because the Church takes average men and makes them great. The cost of leadership is high, but those in any profession or vocation who follow the Master will find that his footsteps lead upward to leadership positions.

Leadership, then, is the one great, common ground that should interest all of our young women, our Aaronic Priesthood youth, and our young adults. Everyone who is faithful, humble and service oriented — who desires to follow in the footsteps of Jesus — will at some time be called to lead. The positions will vary: one may lead in a home teaching district of four or five families, or be an apostle, a bishop, a quorum president, a Relief Society President, head of a Young Women's organization. Somehow it must happen to those who follow the Master without reservation.

Of course, it doesn't come about by one sudden step. Many of us are familiar with the fable about Euclid and the Pharaoh and geometry. It is said that the Pharaoh, entranced by some of the explanations and demonstrations of Euclid, wished to learn geometry, and Euclid undertook to teach him. The Pharaoh studied for a week or ten days and then called in Euclid and told him the process was too slow. He averred that he was a Pharaoh and that hence there must be some shorter road for him. Euclid simply said, "Your majesty, there is no royal road to geometry." This is true also in gaining leadership traits: there's no "easy way" to become a great leader.

In the gospel context, the "where" of our vocations may be as important as the "what." We have a significant problem in the Church in this matter: the philosophy of "Zionitis," as those in outlying areas of the Church would call it. We have in the Church some of the brightest minds of this generation.

I don't believe our Latter-day Saint youth are excelled anywhere collectively. Their opportunities are limited because often, after attending the universities in the West, in the Intermountain area or on the West Coast, and then accepting job offers from across the United States, a few years later they feel a need to return to "Zion."

It would indeed be well for us to counsel our youth to go into "all the world" to share their talent, to set the example, to assume strong and permanent positions of leadership as part of their responsibility of sharing the gospel worldwide.

Truly — if we so direct and lead them — great leaders will rise from the current generation of LDS youth and will evoke the admiration of the world. They will be in politics, in all the vocations, in Church leadership positions. They will be in education, in the professions. They will be lifting themselves to the highest positions in any organization in the world, overcoming the obstacles of life that Angela Morgan so colorfully describes. And they will be found not only in "Zion" but everywhere.

Thomas Jefferson once pointed out that at the same time that life is trying to educate us, it is also *sorting* us. The sorting process classifies each one of us. It will affect each of our lives in one way or another.

In our great attempt to inspire and lift our youth, however, let us not attempt to predestine their lives. Let us instead expose them to as many of life's dimensions as possible, and then as they find what brings them the greatest fulfillment let us encourage them to work untiringly and with great and noble ambition and with a desire for excellence. Whatever vocation or profession they choose, let us also teach them to perform their work with integrity, with understanding, with mercy and justice and empathy for those with whom they relate. In other words, let us help them to become what they were born and meant to be.

The drive for excellence is, of course, very much a part of this process. John W. Gardner in his book *Excellence* suggests that every man who gets to the top must be fiercely motivated. "Motive transcends every other thing in importance," he says. "One of the most precious of all success assets as one strives toward excellence is that quality called drive. It is made up of a keen sense of purpose and indomitability of spirit." Drive and motivation — even fierce motivation — are both qualities that we can teach our youth as they become vocation oriented.

How is a person motivated fiercely? A fierce motivation must come from the individual, and indirectly from the Creator who gave each of us certain ambitions and drives by which we seek to be recognized and to satisfy our physical and spiritual needs. As sensitive, empathetic leaders, we must know our youth well enough to identify these needs and then add those sparks of inspiration and encouragement that propel them — that fiercely motivate them — toward truly gospel-oriented service in each of their lives.

And while that kind of service will require work, we must remember that not all work requires an apron or overalls or work gloves. The artist or the writer works just as hard as the stonemason, the machinist, or the housewife. Mary Roberts Rhinehart, who authored sixty full-length novels, warned that writing is *work*. And I'm sure that Kepler, with his calculations of planetary motion, and Newton, with his meditations on the law of gravitation, would totally agree that *thinking* is work of the heaviest kind.

Many modern influences seek to negate the work ethic, but they are all falsely inspired. Apparent luck or chance may sometimes play their part but are never the major ingredient in true success. I quote from a Royal Bank of Canada newsletter:

> When opportunity for advancement or improvement in your job knocks at your door, she is usually wearing overalls. The pursuit of happiness means work. Freedom means being able to work for things you want. Independence means standing on your own feet free from dependence on others . . . a man has to work because work is an economic necessity — unless he is content to

live on the dole; because it is a social obligation — unless he is content to be graded with the beasts; and because it is a basic human right if he wishes to gain a sense of self-fulfillment.

Nowhere in all the world can we find a more impressive monument to hard work coupled with vision, thrift, and courage than in The Church of Jesus Christ of Latter-day Saints. As we roll up our sleeves and head our youth in the direction of meaningful, fulfilling vocations, let us paint a crystal-clear picture of the Mormon work ethic at its best and inspire our young people to point their futures unmistakably in that direction.

INDEX